To, Seema,

With Respect & Regard.

Vijay

Lj

July 24th 2023.

When Opportunities
Knock
At
Your Door
Open the Door.

Good Luck.

Li J.

TOWARDS THIN AIR

*From Cardiac Bypass
to Everest Bypasses*

VIJAY MALUR

LifeRich Publishing is a registered trademark of The Reader's Digest Association, Inc.

LifeRich Publishing books may be ordered through booksellers or by contacting:

LifeRich Publishing
1663 Liberty Drive
Bloomington, IN 47403
www.liferichpublishing.com
1 (888) 238-8637

ISBN: 978-1-4897-0962-2 (sc)
ISBN: 978-1-4897-0963-9 (hc)
ISBN: 978-1-4897-0961-5 (e)

Library of Congress Control Number: 2016914919

Print information available on the last page.

LifeRich Publishing rev. date: 10/10/2016

DEDICATED TO MY PARENTS MR. RAMANNA AND LATE
MRS. LAKSHMI DEVI RAMANNA FOR THEIR LOVE,
AFFECTION AND DEDICATION IN RAISING OUR FAMILY

THE RELEASE OF THIS BOOK COINCIDES WITH THE 100TH BIRTHDAY
OF MY FATHER WHICH MAKES IT ALL THE MORE JOYOUS

Contents

THE REVIEWS

INSPIRATIONS: – Trip did his heart good, despite coronary disease. Meditation and spirituality provided Vijay with the strength to continue his trek. At one point, he felt the mountain speak to him.

Stacy Hawkins Adams
Freelance Author.
Richmond, VA, USA

Dr. Malur Vijay: Bringing the YMCA mission to the top of the world. YMCA International Peace Flag helped him to spread peace from the top of the world. "The YMCA will bring the children of the world together to form a healthy, peaceful 'world village,'" he said.

Greater Richmond, YMCA
Richmond, VA, USA

I have gone through the book word by word. Why after all this script came to me? Yes, there is a message behind this task. It is a great experience to scale the Great Mountain with the author, who is honest and no way pretentions.

He has turned as a messenger coming from the Himalayas. I had opportunity to see the original paintings (Himalayan) of Messenger both by Nicholar Roerich and Sveteslav Roerich. They had the same soul searching experience while creating these artworks, as they were part of Himalayas. I see a messenger in real life in Dr. Vijay and I am sure he will touch the life of everyone he comes across.

Prof. Choodamani Nandagopal
Art Historian
UK Visiting Nehru Fellow
UNESCO Fellow for Silk Route Studies
Joint Secretary, Indian Art History Congress
Prof. & Head of Academics,
Chitrakala Institute of Advanced Studies (1996-2002)

Through our guide, and Dr. Vijay himself, we were brought to the knowledge that Mr. Vijay completed the Mount Everest Base Camp trek from Lukla to Base Camp in 7 days and 2 and ½ hours. He did the trekking solo, accompanied only by his guide and porter, and without any extra medical assistance or extra oxygen.

Bal Kumar Basnet
Managing Director
For: Parikrama Treks & Expeditions [P] Ltd.
Katmandu, Nepal

FOREWORD

Bypass To Bypasses

Edward A. Peck III, PhD ABPP-CN

I first become acquainted with Malur R. Vijay, MD during the early 1980's when he was a resident in the Department of Physical Medicine at the Medical College of Virginia in Richmond, Virginia. He impressed me then as a person of great energy and positive attitude who merged his religious faith with his powerful intellect and creativity. Even as a student, he had the rare ability to communicate clearly with his patients and to encourage them to strive to overcome their medical problems and resulting personal losses. I had only occasional contact with Malur for more than fifteen years after he left Richmond to begin what eventually became a highly successful Sports Medicine Rehabilitation based medical practice in Boston, Massachusetts. Then he returned to Richmond and appeared as a patient in my private practice and asked that I evaluate him for neuropsychological deficits as the result of an October 1998 head injury and complications from heart disease, which required quadruple-bypass surgery.

As the result of his medical and neuropsychological problems, Malur was forced to cease the practice of medicine. I know that his emotional adjustment to his disability was as difficult for him as it was for anyone who had their life plans irretrievably blocked. Malur eventually saw through his personal catastrophe and was able to see his loss as a positive mechanism for reaching out to help others. Over time, the idea of taking on the personal challenge of climbing the most famous mountain in the world became a means of working toward achieving his own physical, emotional and spiritual rehabilitation as well as empowering other patients around the world to being to take the steps they need to help themselves overcome their losses. I see each incrementally small step towards Malur's personal rehabilitation as being mirrored in his physical steps up the side of a towering Himalayan mountain.

Bypass the Bypass provides a critical message of hope to patients (and their families) who have suffered major losses in their lives. I am honored to call Dr. Malur R. Vijay my friend. Keep climbing!

Edward A. Peck III, PhD, ABPP-CN
Neuro Psychologist
Bremo Road Medical Office Buildings,
Richmond, VA, USA

Shane J. Kraus, M. D

It is a great pleasure for me to write a foreword for Dr. Vijay's book. I have known Dr. Vijay for ten years, when he was a practicing physical medicine and rehabilitation physician. Since then, he has had the misfortune of suffering a traumatic brain injury, heart attack and undergoing coronary artery bypass graft. His strength and personality has led him to a superb recovery, and has surprised me with his vigor, enthusiasm, and recent climb of Mount Everest Base Camp from which he returned safely and regaled us with his stories of the preparation and the journey. I urge all of you to read this book with the idea that everything is possible and as each of you makes your journey through life, use Dr. Vijay's story as your inspiration.

Shane J. Kraus, M.D
Family Practice
7660, Parham Road
Richmond, VA, USA.

Robert H Levitt. M.D

This is an Inspirational story about a person who overcome the Physical and Mental Stresses of Two major Illness to accomplish something truly remarkable. Although Mountain Climbing is not a traditional part of

Cardiac Rehab Program, this story certainly illustrates what can be accomplished.

This is a Must Read Book for anyone who has either been through a major medical crisis or illness, or has been the caregiver for someone for someone with a major Illness.

Robert H Levitt. M.D
Cardiologist,
Henrico Cardiology Associates,
7660, Parham Road,
Richmond, VA, U S A.

Mark R Katz. M.D,

It is unusual for anyone with cardiac History to do that climb. For someone who has been through what he has, it's impressive. He could never accomplish something like that without a positive attitude.

Marc R Katz,
Cardiac Surgeon,
Richmond, VA, U S A.

BEFORE YOU READ THIS BOOK

Through this work of mine, I, present to you the vicissitudes of life encompassing the entire gamut from mundane to extraordinary filled with experiences that are happy, sad, depressing, and exhilarating. This book narrates the events of my life that were successful, disastrous, joyous, tragic, adventurous, and spiritual. You may find a cocktail of all of the above in this story.

In my experience I have come across people who are full of energy, active in life and charismatic have suddenly deteriorated both in their physical and mental status. The fear of having cardiac condition can pull down a person from any heights. In this book I have explained how my pre-cardiac life was and, how my post-cardiac life changed.

In my life, by keeping the physical condition young, the mental condition of accepting the reality of life and to take life one day at a time, I could achieve what I have accomplished. By any means I am not any different from another individual. If an individual like me can handle this, after losing the intellectual memory because of an accident followed by quadruple cardiac bypass surgery, it is my feeling anyone can do it, if only they keep an 'open mind and will' to live their life.

This book will hopefully make the readers take a second look into their life when they think that everything is going wrong for them, whether it is health, wealth, love or anything else. How one relates to this book depends on one's own perception and the events in one's own life.

The Question Is:

Are We All Ready for Something like This?
"Only You Know the Answer"

ACKNOWLEGEMENT

It's customary for an author to thank all the people who have provided help and guidance with this book. As this book is about my life experience, I would begin by thanking people who helped with my life and my work.

I would like to thank my family, my wife Ahalya Vijay, daughter Sahana Vijay and my son Anjan Vijay who are always there after my cardiac bypass surgery and helped me in every way during the post cardiac rehabilitation time. My brother-in-law Mr. Muddu Revanna who helped me immensely during my hard times when I had my head injury, his wife Dr. Brunda Revanna who helped me so much during my post cardiac surgery.

I would like to thank Dr. Marc Katz, my cardiac surgeon, Dr. Robert Levitt, my cardiologist, Dr. Shane Kraus, my family physician, Dr. Edward A Peck, my Neuro-Psychologist, and all the staff of the Henrico doctors Hospital who brought both my physical and mental health to the current state.

I'm grateful to Mrs. Lalitha Thirtha and her daughter Mira Thirtha who pushed me to write this book. My sister Dr. Anjana Ram and my brother-in-law Dr. B.M Ram who went through the script and provided valuable inputs. Dr. Anil K Ram, my nephew who read my first manuscript and gave valuable suggestions. I would like to thank Mr. Vishwanath who helped in the early days of writing this book. Mr. Srinivas Gopal Padmanabhan who helped me in the final corrections and editing.

My son Anjan Vijay who helped me in writing this book using a PC, Ms. Jyothi Rao who let me use her office and helped me find Ms. Padmini my stenographer. My elder brother Mr. M. R. Sivaram and his secretary Ms. Nisha, who arranged all interviews, meeting and lectures.

My sincere thanks to Kishan and Hema Ranji of Richmond, VA for helping me in fine tuning the book.

I would like to thank the Librarians of Twin Hickory branch, Henrico County Public Library and especially Librarian Ms. Hillary Burns for their help to edit and re-edit the book.

I thank the entire team from LifeRich Publishing for their efforts in publishing this book.

BYPASS TO BYPASSES

The very thought of writing down the whole experience sent a thrill, produced a shiver in my body. Even to think that I have successfully completed this is still unbelievable.

Still fresh from the divine experience, when I met my father, I told him that I wanted to disappear into the hills near the city and stay away from humans for some time. I wanted to be a part of nature again. It was still difficult to accept that I was back here. I knew my physical body was here, but I was not here at all. Long after returning from the bosom of Mother Nature, my heart longed to escape the urban jungle to return to the pristine mountains of the Everest. Though physically I'm present it feels that my soul is lost in the mountains of Everest.

I came to Bangalore, India from Nepal where my father and brother lived. Out of the blue one morning I received a call from national Geographic office in New Delhi. They had received a message stating that a sixty-year-old man with quadruple cardiac bypass surgery had reached the Mount Everest Base Camp and that they wanted to know if I could share my fete with the news media. I had no idea what I was getting into when I acceded to their request. The next two days were hectic. I received calls and e-mails from all over the world. Television stations, newspapers, and magazines interviewed me. The level of attention was mind-boggling, yet I managed to handle it with all humility.

I thought about all the changes that happened in the mind. Life taught me that it would take me in its own direction. The interest generated through the media afforded me the wonderful opportunity to deliver lectures so as to inspire people with my experiences.

Following my return from the trek, I have narrated my story many times. Each time after narrating it, I am overpowered by overwhelming stillness and transported to the land of blissful emptiness.

During my stay in Bangalore one early morning when jogging through the park near my father's house I was approached by three elderly gentlemen. One of them looked at me and said, "Thank You." I was perplexed, as I didn't remember having met him before. I asked the gentleman who thanked me, "I don't want to sound rude. Do we know each other?" For which the gentleman replied that he and his friends are cardiac patients and one of them had a triple bypass surgery. He continued that given their conditions they had led a very cautious and sedentary lifestyle, fearing to live a wholesome existence up until three days when they attended my lecture at the Institute World Culture. Since attending the lecture, the gentleman stated that all three of them have decided to "Live life every day and die only once. Do not die every day and never living for a day."

Soon after this moving encounter I came across a highly educated, elderly, spiritual lady, Mrs. Lalitha Thirtha. We struck up an instant friendship. On hearing about my experiences and the encounter with the three gentlemen, Mrs. Lalitha Thirtha impelled me to share my experience with wider audience by writing a book. She is the main source of inspiration for this book.

As a doctor, every time I treated a patient with cardiac problems the patient thinks that his/her life has come to an end, the fun in his/her life is lost forever and that he/she merely exists. I hope that this book will make them look at their lives from a different perspective and live life better than before.

Though I had been writing this book for seven months, it still was incomplete. A couple of weeks before I was ready to take it to the publishers, I took up another unexpected venture. I wanted to meditate for twenty-five hours without a break. For the past ten years, I wanted to do this but for some reason I never could. I started my meditation on Saturday, May 1 2004, at 8:45 AM, and completed it on Sunday, May 2, 2004, at 9:45 AM. This was done at a place called Taponagara, meaning "City of Meditation." This is located on the outskirts of Bangalore, Karnataka, India. The meditation of twenty-five hours was almost comparable to my trek to the Mount Everest Base Camp. During the Everest my body was doing the work and my soul was enjoying the ride. In twenty-five hours of meditation, my soul was doing the work and my body was enjoying the ride. In either case, my body and soul had the ride of a lifetime. Both journeys were exhaustive, spiritual, philosophical, peaceful, and ended in absolute ecstasy, quests in themselves.

Like my trekking experience, this book will be a combination of adventure, disappointment, desperation philosophy, and spirituality, especially for those who think that everything is going wrong in their life. Desperation can come from any type of disappointment or loss. It could be the loss of your health, money, profession, or a family member. It may be a combination of any of the above. What if it is a combination of all of the above? "Impossible! It couldn't be that bad," you exclaim.

Guess what? It can happen.

It happened to me.

I lost my health.

I lost my profession as I lost my ability to practice medicine because of my intellectual memory loss.

I lost my knowledge, all the years of hard work vanished in just one slip.

I lost my wealth. I lost some of my family members and friends too, not in the physical sense, but for all practical purposes.

And it was not once upon a time. It all happened just about five years ago, in 1998. So, what am I doing now?

FATEFUL DAY

Imagine yourself as a successful person in every aspect of life. You have everything in the world you could ask for. You are blessed with affectionate parents, wife, children, loving siblings and friends, a sound profession, enough money, and all the time to spare. Yes, time. Time is the teacher of our lives in this world. One day you are on top of the world, and the next day everything you had worked hard for is gone. This happened in my life. My life was at the helm of everything. Everything changed in one day.

To create the right ambience for our story-telling session, let's get away from here mentally to a mountain peak, a beach, or to the side of a running river. You pick your place. Are you with me?

Practicing physician specializing in Sports Medicine for more than three decades, has a great family, lives in a penthouse with a 23 foot boat in the dock, lots of friends, two offices, drives a Rolls Royce, has a bank balance, a healthy life. Nothing succeeds like success, I was in the process of selling my office and taking it easy, however destiny had its own plans.

That's me on October 5, 1998 when I went to bed that night.

October 6, 1998, everything was gone. How?

It was just a slip, literally. I slipped from the twelfth floor of my building and fell to the eleventh floor. Thud! I ended up with a head injury, resulting in loss of memory, loss of vision, and worse, loss of knowledge. When I regained my orientation, three weeks had passed. Three months had passed by the time I could comprehend what was going on around me. My bank had foreclosed on my office, taken possession of all the equipment and receivable bills and confiscated every other asset associated with my business. My lifetime earnings were all gone. Just vanished. Does that sound incredible, Just believe me for now.

I am here to tell you how it all happened. The day wasn't any different from all other days. I had finished meeting my patients in one of the offices and was heading to the other. While driving to the other office I remembered that I had left my clothes in the laundry room, which was on the twelfth floor in my apartment building. I decided to go to my apartment to get the clothes as the apartment maintenance staff closed the laundry room by 8 pm. Instead of using the elevator, I decided to climb to the 12th floor. On reaching the laundry room I collected all my clothes and started to climb down the stairs. On taking the very second step, I faltered and had a pratfall. I managed to get up and started to climb down when I staggered and fell head long. I hit the concrete floor and fell unconscious. I regained my consciousness partially. I was confused and in pain. I wasn't sure how long I had passed out I wasn't able to move.

Time passed. The thought of me lying on the floor with no chance of being found, as no one used the stairs, scared me. This propelled me to crawl to a door that was 2 feet away from where I was lying. I do not remember how I managed to open the door, crawled into the corridor, and faint again. It is amazing how the human body works in times of extreme circumstances.

When I opened my eyes, I was inside a hospital and a doctor was asking something. I felt as if I were in a tunnel. The happenings around me were dream like. On gaining consciousness, I was told that a neighbor had found me in the corridor and had called for the ambulance. The doctor told me that my shoulders and hip were injured, broken bones, but the worst thing was that I had closed head injury, meaning concussion of the brain. Further, I had lost vision in my right eye and my pupils were dilated and fixed, meaning that they were not reacting to light as they would under normal circumstances.

I ended October 6, 1998 on a hospital bed. I continued to drift between conscious and unconscious state. It was two weeks before things started to stabilize in which time I was moved to Virginia from Massachusetts for treatment and recuperation.

I was in a state of stupor. There was nothing I could consciously do to come out of it. But the dessert was yet to be served. To add to disasters that had befallen me, I had another diagnosis with not one but four blockages in the coronary arteries! I was told I had to undergo immediate quadruple bypass surgery. It felt as if I were hit by lightning. No way can this happen to a person who followed a healthy lifestyle all through his life. I resigned to fate. So I submitted myself to it on December 8, 1998.

Slowly, but steadily, my condition improved. I was not one of those persons who brooded over things that did not go my way. I always looked at life with a philosophical attitude. I took whatever came to me in my life with a smile and I bid goodbye to whatever left me.

Some may call it fatalism, but I disagree. For me, it was the acceptance of reality and overcoming the sense of ego that is within every one of us. After a series of tests, doctors told me that I was unfit to practice medicine given the memory loss suffered due to the head injury. The doctors also warned me against performing any manual work because of cardiac problem.

A hypothetical question:

Can you imagine yourself in the same situation that I described? What would be your reaction? Are you in any way prepared for such a series of unexpected events? How would you cope with things?

Just close your eyes. Imagine for a few seconds that the events of these two months of my life happened to you. God forbid! Let me pray that such a thing never happens to you or anyone else. But yes, it can happen to anyone, at any time, and at any place. Agreed?

EARLY DAYS

I was born on *September 19, 1944*, at Bangalore, India. My father, Mr. M. R. Ramanna, who at 98 is fiercely independent and still performs all his daily activities with no assistance, retired as Director of Physical Education in the University of Mysore. From him I imbibed the valuable lesson of doing one's duty without worrying about the fruits and to take life with a smile even when things do not go the way we wish. My late mother Mrs. Lakshmi Devi Ramanna, who was a Member of State Legislative Assembly for over twenty years, taught me to stand up for any cause that was right and to fight for justice regardless of who I faced. She imparted to me the importance of bestowing love and compassion to fellow human beings particularly towards the less fortunate.

Though my parents could afford to send me and my siblings to private school that solely catered to the rich and the famous, they decided to send us to the public school. This exercise was to enable us to learn and understand the opportunities and privileges we enjoyed over our less-fortunate schoolmates who came from underprivileged homes. This experience at that young age was an eye opener as it called to the attention of the disparities that existed in society. We stayed in the public school till we completed our middle school after which we were admitted to St. Joseph's High school, a private school. It was Catholic mission school where I was exposed to Christianity, a religion different from the one we practiced at home.

Even as a teenager, I was adventure loving. When I was about 14 years of age, I wanted to go on a biking tour to a nearby hill station that was about 40 miles away from my city with my friends. My parents did not like my idea and refused to let me go. The call of the mountain was very strong. I wanted to go to the mountains even though my parents had not given me permission. Guess what I did? On the planned morning, I left for the biking tour at 3 a.m. after leaving a note to my parents informing them that I was going on the bike tour and begging them to forgive me for disobeying them. I did enjoy the trip and it was my first adventure with mountains. After the successful completion of the trip, I was very scared to face my parents. My father was peeved with my disobedience. He reprimanded me for my action of not obeying his words. My father himself being of adventurous nature could not hide his appreciation, which I did not fail to notice from the sparkle in his eyes. But my mother was very upset with my behavior and she remained that way for a few days.

I always aspired to become a doctor. Therefore on graduating from school, I joined the medical college of Bangalore University, India. In 1969, I graduated as a bachelor of medicine and surgery. Shortly thereafter, I was married in 1971, soon came the births of my daughter and son. My marriage was arranged by my parents in the traditional Indian way. My wife was solely interested in the welfare of our family during the earlier days. She went along with whatever decisions I took in life. Whether it was right or wrong I cannot comment. But that was the way in earlier days. Now things have changed and are different. For better or worse? I do not know. But one thing remains the same, I have been happy and at peace all my life!

In 1972, I decided to leave the shores of India to pursue higher education. I moved to England, where I qualified as an orthopedic surgeon. I was involved in medical research and acquired patens for some medical equipment in Britain. As I was getting established as a successful orthopedic surgeon in Britain, I had wanted to go back to India and render services to the deserving in my motherland. But destiny had its own plans. I decided to move to the United States of America at the behest of my extended family who convinced me to set up medical practice in the United States of America. So I left England in 1979 for the United States.

The euphoria of moving to America and raking in the 'moolah' died a natural death when I realized that I had to start all over again like a fresh graduate starting from a residency program, fellowship, and passing all exams. My goodness! Ten years after finishing medical school, it was really hard for the brain to absorb things. I had to compete with the best among the local graduates and foreign graduates from all over the world. The one thing that stood by me was my never-say-die attitude. On coming to the USA, I along with my family moved in with my sister who was living in Virginia. My sister locked me up in a room and asked me to just focus on the exams. I was allowed outside of my room only during lunch and dinner. The 28 days of solitary confinement paid off and I passed all the exams, following which I completed my residency in Physical Medicine and Rehabilitation.

Being a resident doctor those days meant long hours of work. In those days young doctors worked very long hours. I remember often going to the hospital on Friday mornings and returning Monday evenings. What a drain such heavy workloads were on young doctors! The residents had to stay on call on the weekends, which started on Friday mornings and went on, seemingly endlessly, until Monday evenings. It is such a relief that there is a limit of forty hours per week on the shifts nowadays.

After residency, I did fellowship in spinal cord injuries, as part of which I went to the renowned Harvard University to do non-surgical sports medicine training. On the successful completion, I joined the McGuire Veterans Medical Center Richmond, VA, as Unit Chief, Department of spinal cord injuries.

IMPERMANENCE OF LIFE

During my tenure at McGuire Veterans Medical Center, I met an elderly man admitted as a quadriplegic patient, who has lost complete control of his body below the neck. This man was 68 years old, had worked hard as a dentist and had retired only a year earlier. He wanted to enjoy the last years of his life with his wife travelling around the world. However, life had a different script written for him, now he was bed-and wheelchair-bound for the rest of his life, with no control over his breathing. The unmistakable irony of life cannot be overlooked. Why did God change his life? What is the lesson this man has to learn from his now dependent life? About a week later I came across another quadriplegic patient with the same degree of affliction. He was a six-and-a-half-foot-tall, handsome youth, just 32. His father, a poor postal worker, had worked against all odds to give his son a good education. The son fulfilled his father's dreams. He graduated from the Harvard Medical College and completed the residency program. Now, he was on the threshold of his professional life as an orthopedic surgeon, with all the hopes and expectations of a very bright future. However, that was not to be. There was a different timetable set for him. One day when driving his brand new Porsche he was involved in an accident rendering him a quadriplegic. That was the end of his career and dreams.

Looking at these two men, I could not help asking myself: Who is in control? Is it the Egoistic me? Is it the Fate? Was it just a Coincidence? Or is it the Timetable of Destiny?

However, what almost any human being would still assert is, "I am in control." No one but Christopher Reeves the on screen Superman could epitomize the reality of life. He was the one of most successful Hollywood star with worldwide following who met with an accident while riding a horse. The accident turned this star an active man all his life into a quadriplegic. This was as bad as a 1000 voltage electric jolt. Life did not end here for him. Christopher Reeves instead of sulking and confining himself to the four walls of his home started to lend his voice to bring to the forefront the issues faced by people with spinal injuries which till then were not taken seriously. Until the day he died he was fighting to get political approval and funding for stem cell research, a raging and controversial subject in contemporary social America. He by his unflinching service overcame and transcended his disability. He is a true inspiration for all to take life head long despite the odds.

Every one of us wants to be competitive, successful, and famous. I do not mean that anything is wrong with all this. Nevertheless, I believe in a sportive attitude, give your best and do the job but accept the outcome with a balanced mind. Otherwise, we could turn our lives into misery. If this spirit could be imbued into every walk of our life, the world would be a better place.

I had now lived in Richmond for 6 years. During this time I decided to augment my income by creating sources other than medical profession and ventured into business. I financed a couple of businesses though not participating in day-to-day affairs. Though I did not make much money from these ventures, I did not lose any either. Because of these ventures, I fully realized, "Money is important but money is not everything in life." I learned that any person who values money alone is perhaps a most lonely and unhappy person.

After about eight years in the department of spinal cord injury, I decided to move out into my own specialty practice. Therefore, in 1992 I went to Boston, Massachusetts, which is 600 miles from Virginia, and established a sports medicine center. But I could not take my family along because we did not want to disturb the education of my two college-going kids. My wife and children continued to live in Virginia. Most of my friends disapproved this move stating that I needed to stay with the family. Once a month I drove to Virginia to be with the family. This went on for another eight years. Reflecting now, I wonder did I do all that out of my free will, or was Destiny controlling my life?

After about eight years in Boston when I took stock of life, my children were successful in their life, I had three hospital affiliations, lived in a penthouse by the sea with a boat in the dock and a Rolls Royce in the garage. God had given me everything. What more could I ask for?

However, contentment was quickly giving way to new plans. I felt a strong urge to come out of this mechanical life and do something else. It was time for better things, I thought. I decided to put my practice and office up for sale. I decided to move back to Virginia. That was my plan. But ... ...Just a slip of the foot and all my plans went awry. After the head injury, I was moved to Virginia not as free as I'd wanted, but for treatment and recuperation. So frustrating! However, I was yet to understand the full implications of the accident.

TURN OF EVENTS

Many surprises were in store. I learned after undergoing a series of test that I had loss of memory and vision in the right eye too was affected badly. The doctors told me emphatically: "You will not be competent to practice medicine anymore." This put me in the category of the mentally and physically disabled. My intellectual memory was gone; I had lost all my lifetime experience and knowledge. I lost my ability to practice medicine the only job I had done all my life. I was confused about my future. I was grappling with questions like: What was next? Where was I heading? I did not possess any other skill for making a living.

Before I could gather my wits to find an answer, my primary physician came back and said, "Dr. Vijay, we will need to take one more EKG because I think there is some abnormality. I just want to be sure." He referred me to a cardiologist. A cardiac stress test was done but it was inconclusive. Then they performed an angiogram. I was also watching the screen, just a little curious. What I saw should have stopped my heart, if it had been made of any weaker stuff. All the four major blood vessels were almost blocked!! The overall average blood supply to the heart was very minimal.

My cardiologist blurted out in disbelief: "Hey Vijay, do you see what I see?" "…Yes". "You know what it means, right?" "Yes." "You are sitting on a ticking time bomb." Of course I was. A single block itself could trigger a fatal heart attack. But four of them! The prognosis did not bode well. The course of treatment was not an easy one. A critical surgery with many inherent risks had to be performed. I remained calm, I was not scared, but my family was shocked. After discussions with the cardiac surgeon, a date was scheduled to perform a triple bypass surgery. However, on the day of the surgery doctors knew it had to be a quadruple bypass and not a triple bypass.

I was on the verge of bankruptcy due to loss of profession, as I could not practice medicine anymore because of the head injury sustained three months earlier. Now I had to go through cardiac surgery! As a physician I was aware of the risks from cardiac bypass surgery especially as I was still recovering from the head injury. Then the postsurgical complications had to be taken into consideration. Further, this surgical procedure itself could add on to the complications from my head injury.

I was not afraid of death or surgery. Once again, I geared up to face the realities of this second battle like a warrior. From the medical standpoint, I was in the best hospital care, treated by best doctors in the world. I was ready to face the challenge thrown by life. Actually, as I was taken into the operating room I could not help smiling. Nothing could take the peace of mind away from me. It was God's greatest gift to me.

The cardiac surgery was successful and the post cardiac rehabilitation went well though it was very tiring and painful.

THE LESSONS

I was lost. I was unable to think coherently. I had no clear and precise thinking. The power of reasoning was almost extinct. My mental faculties reached a nadir coupled with bad sight in the right eye. I was helpless and was overwhelmed by turn of events, in particular about the physical and mental disabilities. After two years of trauma, I began to understand and accept my situation. There was nothing I could do but to embrace the present. I just looked at my situation and smiled. I have come to believe that "Destiny's timetable" is framed the moment conception takes place. We humans want to erase it and rewrite the way we want things to be, but that will never happen.

Having accepted the reality of the disabilities that were the result of the accident was one thing. Now I had to face the financial difficulties, due to loss of memory I was unfit to perform in the medical profession, the only job for which I was trained. Given the cardiac conditions I was not fit to perform any manual job. My income completely stopped and I was not able to manage the recurring mounting expenses. As a result, banking institutions foreclosed on my practice and receivables. My disability insurance policy that went into effect only after three months and barely covered my basic expenses.

I learned a lot about relationships and friendships during this time. It was an eye-opening experience. It is said that a best friend is one who will never leave our side come what may. We should consider ourselves fortunate if we have such friends who are with us in the time of need. Many of my friends were by my side when I underwent these miseries and helped me in many ways.

At the time when I had the fall, before I hit the floor, in that fraction of the second my whole life went before me, I lost my conscious when I hit the floor. After the fall, and the resultant head injury I had come to believe that we all have been bestowed with two great friends, i.e. life and death. Though many people consider death as morbid it ought to be celebrated. Death represents end of this journey and start of a new adventure. The only reason we fear death is due to the fear of the unknown. However when we read the accounts of people who had experienced, Near-Death-Experience (NDE), it dispels this fear. People who experienced NDE talked about a loving light and a desire to stay in the light not wanting to leave. However as their time on earth was not over, they were sent back. After their NDE these people lost their fear of death and looked forward to it to happen.

I too had experienced NDE and would not disagree nor differ with the experiences of others. I realized that my physical body was irrelevant. I was covered by this wonderful feeling, which oozed with love and divinity. I had no desire to leave this state of mind. I realized my true self. However this stay in the divinity was short-lived as I was asked to leave, as it was not my time. Despite the stubbornness on my part not to leave "they" prevailed. I came back to this physical body. This experience gave me more strength. It made me realize that everything was ephemeral. What mattered are the experiences we undergo in this life.

After the NDE, I completely started to accept my situation. All that mattered from then on was to enjoy the experiences. I no longer had fear of death. All uncertainties about life faded away. I wanted to die but I had no control and was sent back. That showed that I had to enjoy the experience instead of attempting to alter the situation. There was no way I could get back my intellectual memory and knowledge. I accepted that I could never practice as a doctor, the only job I had done all my life.

I realized that life of a human being is like a pearl on a leaf in a mighty river. Though the egoistic pearl might think it is in control, in reality the pearl's existence depends on the mercy of the mighty river. This does not mean that we have to give up everything and stop aspiring. We still have to live life and aspire for things; however, we should stop to identify ourselves with our actions and just enjoy the experience. Once acceptance sets in, life becomes blissful.

ROAD TO RECOVERY

It took me nearly two years to overcome the effects of the twin traumas. Due to my life experience, I wanted to be of some service to the society in whatever way I could, taking into consideration both my mental and physical limitations. I was constantly monitored on both my physical body and mental faculties. My physical body almost limped back to normal bit till today my intellectual memory is damaged. I lost the knowledge I had strived for all my life.

In the year 2000, I started volunteering for 'Meals on Wheels,' which caters food to lonely old people who cannot shop or cook for themselves. Many elderly men and women aged between 75 and 95 accepted me as their son. The look in their eyes when they received food was gratifying which equaled no reward. I felt this experience to me was more fulfilling. In the past I had been a doctor that was considered to be a noble profession, but a fee was charged for the service. A true service is one where you serve someone unconditionally.

I volunteered to be a big brother to some less fortunate children. I found joy in assisting them in shopping, taking them to the library, and teaching them how to be good citizens. Life rolled on for about three years. As I approached sixty, with lots of time at my disposal, I started to practice Meditation for longer durations that helped me physically and spiritually. As time passed my physical health and the vision in my right eye improved. The right pupil started reacting to light.

Once again I could resume my normal activities though there was no improvement with respect to loss of memory. I still could not recollect many things. Pondering over the turn of events and the state of mind, I could have lost my sanity. Because of my eastern philosophical upbringing I retained it.

There was plenty of time on hand so I decided to learn computers. When I was in my practice I was so ignorant about computers and was barely able to use them without my secretary. With the help of my son Anjan, I learnt to surf the Net and discovered the world of Internet.

Born and raised as a Hindu, my first thought was to undertake a pilgrimage in India. As per ancient Hindu tradition, a man should spend his later part of his life on pilgrimage. Having my education at a catholic institution in Bangalore, India, I had learned about Christianity and visited churches. Some of my best friends were Muslims, which provided me with an opportunity to be exposed to Islam. So after being exposed to various religions, I believed in Albert Einstein's words, "True religion is real living; living with all one's soul, with all one's goodness and righteousness" which I practice and taught my children too. A strong desire welled up in me to travel around the world despite my questionable health-physical and mental coupled with limited availability of funds.

A couple of years after my disability I had holidayed in Europe with a group of close friends. Particularly the Alps, in Switzerland captivated me. It was so beautiful. I felt like the mountain peaks were beckoning me to be a part of them.

Later, I visited the Canadian Rocky Mountains. My God, what great mountains these are! The Rockies made the Alps look tiny! It appeared that only a hundred Alps put together could equal the great Rocky Mountains. I went up in a cable car to the top of one of the peaks in Banff, up to an altitude of 10,000 feet. It was a great view. Perched on the mountain top, I could see the morning mist rise up from the ground. It was like a cloud rising from the earth to the sky – truly heavenly! I told a friend who had accompanied me that this peak was 10,000 feet whereas Mount Everest was 29,000 feet – three times higher. Would it be that difficult to go to Mount Everest? It was an ignorant, immature statement. Later on my way to the base camp of Mount Everest, I apologized to the Himalayas for the fool hardy statement.

After the visit to the Rocky Mountain, I traveled to the Caribbean islands. These islands were a beauty unto themselves. The people were very friendly, simple and I was also very impressed with their adaptation to nature. In the midst of mighty Atlantic Ocean, these tiny islands look so helpless, but Mother Ocean takes care of them like babies. What a harmony between these islands and the mighty ocean.

My urge for travelling was always present and I was looking for any opportunity to travel, which could fit my physical, mental and financial limitations. All these memories of visiting various mountains flooded my mind. The urge to travel to mountains was there in my mind all the time. I always believed that "There is a destiny's timetable governing all our activities, but we try to erase it or try to work around it, but it seldom can be changed."

One evening while I was browsing on the Internet I joined a chat room pertaining to travel. As the conversation was veering around the topic of mountains, I felt like sharing my little experience with another person in the chat room (whose identity I do not know). I said in a know-it-all manner that the great Canadian Rocky Mountains would equal one hundred Alps Mountains put together. As soon as I typed this, I got a message back from this person "Take one thousand Rocky Mountains and put it in one place that will only be a part of the great Himalayan Range". This statement triggered me to decide I should go to Mt. Everest. This was my destiny's invitation. At that moment I could see the timetable of my destiny.

All I had to do was close my eyes to feel the invisible invitation to be at the foot of Mount Everest, the "Sagara Matha". In Nepalese Mt. Everest is known as "Sagara Matha" which means "Goddess of the Sky". I made the decision that "My pilgrimage is towards Mount Everest Base Camp" (MEBC). I did not bother to ponder on the question "How?" I told myself that details could always be worked out later.

During my research I did find a trekking agency "Parikrama Trekking & Expeditions", Katmandu, Nepal that offered good package deals for trekkers to MEBC. I made the decision to choose them as the trekking agency for my MEBC pilgrimage.

THE HURDLES TO JUMP

There were three major hurdles, fiscal, physical, and personal. The financial situation was grave. I had borrowed from financial institutions, family and friends. I had to repay these amounts. Due to the soaring real estate, the value of my home increased. I wanted to refinance my house and pay off all the debts. However, no mortgage company wanted to refinance due to bad credit, which was the result of fore closure of my business. Finally, one company, on hearing my story, agreed to refinance. God! What a feeling it was! It is such a relief when you know that you do not have any personal debts. It was a great relief for my family. I had cleared one hurdle.

Physically, my condition was improving, and my meditation helped me control my heart rate and calm my mind. I had no acute distress, and after regular medical checkups, my primary physician told me that I was in good physical shape hut I can do nothing about my loss of intellectual memory. My second hurdle was clear.

Third and the final hurdle was to conquer myself and convince my family. Conquering myself was not difficult, as I had always enjoyed living adventurously. Convincing my wife was difficult as she tried everything possible to prevent me undertaking this trip. She even joined others to discourage me from pursuing this venture. My daughter, Sahana, a dentist, was like any other daughter, and was emotional. She said I can no longer act as a hero with my physical and mental conditions. Only my son encouraged me to go ahead with my plans. He wished me a safe trip and enjoyable journey. My friends discouraged me in many ways. I knew that they were my well-wishers and were concerned about my safety and health, but I still was firm on my decision to go towards Mount Everest Base Camp.

Immediately I paid 50% of the deal to "Parikrama Trekking & Expeditions", Katmandu. Nepal, and the balance was due when I landed at Katmandu. Once I made this financial commitment, a pleasant shudder went through my body. All these events took place between March and April 2003. The trekking agency advised me that the best time to visit Base Camp would be between April and August. I decided to be there in May 2003 I wanted to be at the Base Camp on a full moon day that happened to be May 16, 2003.

SELF-TAILORED TRAINING PROGRAM

All my life I had led an active life and had participated things like scuba diving, sky diving, white water rafting and hot air ballooning but never done any trekking. I realized that climbing mountains required real stamina and training. I had no experience in trekking big peaks.

I contacted the Trekking agency at Katmandu and asked them if there was any special exercise program that I should do. I was told to be in fit condition to trek about eight to ten miles per day. Other than that there was no other special training mentioned to go to the MEBC. As I had been a sports medicine doctor, my experience helped me to tailor the training schedule to prepare for the journey. I also researched through Internet to gather information regarding preparations for spending time in high altitude. However, there were no resources which specifically catered people with cardiac problems.

During a typical day my schedule was walking 10 miles a day and climbing one hundred floors on the Stairmaster at my health club. I also started taking cold water showers and gradually switched over to ice-cold showers. To date, I still take ice-cold showers. Through meditation I developed control over respiration and sustained calmness of mind. This training routine Continued until the day of my departure for Nepal via India. Just before I left Richmond I had my health checkup with both my Family Physician and cardiologist. They gave me a clean bill of health and were impressed with my condition in particular the cardiac health.

My dietary requirements were minimal. I stopped eating breakfast about thirty years ago. Later my diet was reduced to one meal a day and seven years ago I started living on one meal on alternate nights. I had trained my body to sustain my daily activities with one meal every other night.

By nature I loved the seasonal cold weather with snow, as cold always kept me awake and active. The eight years that I had spent in Boston had prepared me to the weather of extreme cold conditions. I had no trouble there. But the cold weather conditions of Boston, which I was accustomed to, was never as harsh as that of the Himalayas that I would endure.

As the preparations went on and D-day approached I could feel my inner calmness. My mind increasingly started lingering on philosophical and spiritual thoughts though there was no conscious attempt from my side. I could not help attributing this to the Himalayas with which I had fallen deeply in love. It is a great journey in any-body's lifetime. If going to the Base Camp itself produced this feeling in me, who can imagine the feeling of those reaching the peak?

I made a list of the things I would need for the trek. I did not want to take anything unnecessary. At the same time I did not want to omit anything I might need. I packed the basic medical products such as Ace wraps, bandage, antibiotics, analgesic, and insect repellent along with three pairs of trekking boots. I also packed some small surgical tools to use in the event of an absolute emergency.

Once all the preparations for the trip were complete, I visited my near and dear ones spread across the USA. They had mixed feelings about the trip. I could see their concern especially regarding my health problems. However, they all bestowed their best wishes and prayed for my safe return. Some of the adventurous types even wished they could join me. I also received requests for special souvenirs. One friend wanted 'a piece of Mount Everest,' another asked for the "peace prayer flag" from the Himalayas. The third one wanted me to meet the Yeti, the Abominable Snowman, and get a lock of hair from him! One of the most heartfelt requests came from an elderly woman whom I knew from 'Meals on Wheels' who wanted to touch my hand that had touched Mt. Everest after my return from Mount Everest Base Camp. Such unusual requests with spiritual sentiments set me thinking. The value of material things suddenly appeared to shrink. I wondered how the Himalayas could send such spiritual vibrations to these individuals. But were they just my friends, or were they involved with me in this endeavor in some way?

The original plan was to go to Nepal (from America) first, finish the trek and then go to India to visit my father and extended family. However, the inner voice told me to visit India and then go on the trek. My American friends strongly endorsed this view. Therefore, I changed the itinerary. I thought there must be some purpose behind this, which I could not comprehend. The day came when it was time to bid farewell to my family. Some of my close friends were there to bid me farewell. I left America during the last week of April 2003, flew to Bangalore. India. After spending ten days with my father and my elder brother, I left for Katmandu, Nepal on May 7, 2003.

START OF THE JOURNEY

On May 7, 2003. I left Bangalore early in the morning with the blessings of my father and elder brother and best wishes of many friends. The baggage consisted of trekking-related equipment, boots, and warm clothing. I had $2250 USD. 20000 Indian Rupees and a credit card. I had already paid $1000 to the trekking agency in advance from America, the balance of $1400 to be paid upon on the arrival at Katmandu, Nepal. This was a package deal of $2400 for the entire trip. This included all the trekking gear, food, lodging, and air flight from Katmandu to Lukla — the starting point of the trek.

From Bangalore it was necessary to go via New Delhi, as there were no direct flights to Katmandu. We landed at New Delhi at 9:30 am, IST, where I spent the whole day, as the flight to Katmandu was at 7 pm IST. In the ensuing period I started to read the book "Siddhartha" by Herman Hesse. I had read this book before but I felt compelled to read it again. It was so soothing and comforting. The book revolves around two characters Siddhartha and Govinda. I realized when reading the book, at the airport, that the goals of Siddhartha and Govinda were one and the same though they chose different paths in their quest for truth. I started to ponder. Then what was my goal? What was my path?

These thoughts went through my mind. But they did not bother me too much. There was calm in me just thinking about my impending quest of the Himalayas.

I had a sense of Deja vu since the beginning of the journey. I felt that I already knew the places that I was yet to visit and that I was only taking this journey in a different physical form. Though I was sitting in the airport lounge, I was hardly aware of anyone. I had merged and felt I was becoming a part of Universal Spirituality.

Normally most people would have become restless and groaned about waiting in a busy airport even for a half an hour let alone the whole day, but I had no problems spending time at the airport as it gave me an opportunity to observe people. Now everything was different. The whole day seemed to have gone in a jiffy was that because I was heading to the foot of Mount Everest? "Sagara Matha" literally means 'Mother of Ocean very intriguing. What an epithet the local people have given to this mountain on top of the world! It speaks lot about their philosophy and culture. Sky is referred to as the ocean and the Mountain as the mother. Mount Everest can also be seen in a different way: Mount Everest is the Mother of Ocean of knowledge, philosophy, culture, civilization, humanity, and spirituality.

The flight left New Delhi at 7 pm and reached Katmandu at 9:30 pm. When I came out of the flight, saw a board displaying my name. Two gentlemen from Parikrama Treks and Expeditions were waiting. I immediately recognized Mr. Kumar, Parikrama Managing director (whose picture I had seen in the brochure), walked them and said "Hello." The person with Kumar was his assistant Mr. Raj. The latter was going to be my guide for next two or three days in Katmandu Valley. Within no time I had taken a strong liking for them. The way they communicated with me, whether through words or action- a simple gesture like picking up my kit — all impressed me very much. They had created a great impression in my mind about their small country. Everything about Nepal: The people, culture, and their hospitality struck a positive note. My itinerary would start the next day. They took me to a three star hotel but it rivaled any five-star hotel I had ever visited in America.

The next day we went through trekking expenses. I signed some forms. I paid the balance of $1.400 to Kumar to complete the deal. I still had $850 left with me. I thought it would be a good idea to have some Nepali Rupees. I got $300.00 changed into Nepali Rupees. The Dollar conversion was $1.00 for every 70.00 Rupees. This gave me a total of 21,000 Nepali Rupees. I also learned I would be the only trekker in the group as others had backed out due to fear of SARS.

They had arranged an air-conditioned car with a good driver, whose name was Sunny. I was amazed to find them all conversing in good English. Kumar was from a family of Sherpas and had a High School Diploma. Raj was a graduate of a college in Darjeeling, India, one of the best colleges in India. It is a dream for every Indian parent to send his or her children to this college. I hit the road with Raj and Sunny.

Before we started on the city tour, I came to know that the US embassy was close by. We went to the US embassy, to inform them that I was going on a trek to the Mount Everest Base Camp. All US citizens going on treks are advised to do so by the visa office in Washington. D.C. The purpose of this is to keep track of trekkers, and follow up in case it was necessary. After furnishing the details, we proceeded to see the city of Katmandu and Katmandu Valley.

NEPAL

Katmandu is a very busy, overcrowded, dusty, smoke-polluted city, like many of its Indian counterparts it is an art to drive its narrow streets. Almost everybody walks in the middle of the streets and so do the animals. I noticed every driver was engaged in a continuous unspoken communication with the drivers of motorbikes, trucks, rickshaws, as well as pedestrians, cows, sheep, chickens, and any birds that flew in. Yet, like a river, the traffic stream keeps flowing in its own style, at its own pace, with only a few small bumps and dings on the cars.

As we drove, I was pleased to see attractive children going to schools dressed in their uniforms. I know this is a most common sight in India, so there seems nothing remarkable about it to Indians. This is striking to me because in the US, with the exception of some private institutions, most of the schools do not prescribe uniforms, and the children are free to wear whatever they like. Thus, the difference between the wealthy and poor children becomes immediately apparent. I always felt that this might affect the children's psyche.

In Nepal widespread poverty is quite visible. At the same time the people are not famished and they do not look starved. You can see peace and calmness in their cheerful smiling faces. I was amazed to see the contentment that vibrates in their faces in the midst of poverty.

After visiting the US embassy we went to North Buddha Stupa, which is like a mausoleum for Lord Buddha; also like a temple or a shrine. People go there to pray, meditate, or spend some quiet time. When I arrived there, the idea struck me that all these events and experiences were precious. I realized the memory were to be cherished for a lifetime. So many things were happening in quick succession, that unless I recorded the immediately they would all fade from my memory. My memory retention was still faulty. I never had the habit of keeping a journal of day-to-day happenings. However, given the issues with my memory now I decided to jot down everything. This way I could precisely remember where I had been and what I had seen. Before entering the Stupa, I went to a nearby shop to get a diary. The very first one that I saw attracted me. The book had an antique look; the paper appeared to be brittle but was not really so. Most importantly a golden colored Buddha sat on the cover. I felt as if he was telling me. "Take me home with you; your very life will change from now on" I bought the diary.

Looking at the Stupa, the very first image that went through my mind was that of Gautama Buddha sitting in deep meditation. As we entered it, I felt an inexplicable peace and calmness dawn on me. The Stupa constructed in the shape of meditating Gautama Buddha and an enclosure was later built around it. Therefore the Stupa was more of a monument than temple. From the middle of the Stupa building rises the dome. This dome is rectangular and faces all four directions.

On the Top of North Buddha Stupa – Katmandu.

On Top of North Buddha Stupa

There are a pair of eye painted on each of its four sides. The eyes have a deep penetrating look. I kept staring at them. When you are in places like this, you cannot help but become spiritual and philosophical.

Man's spirituality begins when he is in the sitting position. Self, which is in contact with the earth, travels upwards through our body, starting from the contact point on earth and ascending upwards on the back of the spine towards the head. Eventually, one sees the truth of the world through those pairs of eyes. 'Those pairs of eyes represented the inner eye of every human being.' A person can see the truth of this materialistic world through one's Inner Eyes. This was the thought that went through my mind.

After sitting on the Stupa for some time, we took a stroll around it. We walked on the roof of the Stupa. This was unusual for me, and in fact uncomfortable, as it is against Hindu beliefs and customs to walk over a temple. Anyway, I reconciled to the local custom and after going around a little, went to the top, found a quiet place, and sat down. I sat there very quietly, and did nothing, thought nothing, felt nothing, looked at nothing and I was nothing. With no physical movement and no mental thought, I was able to go into an absolute thoughtless zone. I had become a part of the Stupa. How long this went on, I do not know.

When I opened my eyes, the thought that came to mind was the definition of poverty. To most people, poverty only means lack of wealth and money. However, there are so many kinds of poverty: poverty of Wealth, Honesty, Purity, Simplicity, Forgiveness, Charity, Love and Compassion. At the same time, there is a treasury of wealth in all of the above virtues. So if we take a total score of these values in an individual, we will know how poor or rich he is. Obviously, 'Wealthy' does not refer to someone with money only. This reminds me of the statements that my professor of surgery (During our college days) used to make. "The eye cannot see what the mind does not know" and "Beauty lies in the eye of beholder". The beauty lies in the eye of the beholder to see the Virtues of Poverty & Wealth in each individual. With these thoughts we left the Stupa.

From the Buddha Stupa we went on to many other temples. Architecturally, every temple looks more beautiful than the other. At each of those places there is lot of visible filth, but still none of this would be visible to many of the pilgrims, as they can perceive only the spirituality.

Later, we went to Hanuman Dhoka (The gates of Hanuman) also known as Durbar Square of the ancient city of Katmandu. This large square is the historic seat of the Nepalese Royalty. The Square, with its old temples and palaces, epitomizes the religious and cultural life of the people. It is here where Kings of Nepal are crowned. Within the Durbar Square, we visited a three-tiered pagoda style temple built by King Mahendra Malla in 1549. This magnificent temple of goddess Talejubhawani speaks volumes on the Buddhist Architecture.

Hanuman Dhoka houses the renowned "Kumari Ghar" (The house of the Kumari or virgin or the living goddess) Kumari Ghar was built in 1757 during the reign of King Jayaprakash Malla. This is a three-floor brick structure which has intricately carved wooden lattice windows all around it and houses the caretakers of the Kumari, or Kumarini. The house is guarded by two enormous white stone lions. The fusion of Buddhist architecture and Hindu ornamentation has a significant presence cannot be missed by one's eyes. The Kumari Devi is a young girl (selected with 32 predetermined qualities) who lives in the building known as the Kumari Ghar. From time immemorial the practice of worshipping an ordinary pre-pubescent girl as a source of supreme power has been an integral part of Hinduism. To catch a glimpse of the Kumari, one must enter into the courtyard of the Kumari Ghar, known as the Kumari Chowk. Directly across from the entrance of the courtyard you can see the intricate windows on the third floor where the Kumari herself occasionally passes by to regard her worshippers. According to a popular belief, Kumari possesses unlimited spiritual powers and protects people from demons and evil spirits. I did not have a chance for a glimpse of Kumari.

For lunch we went to an authentic Nepali restaurant situated on a third floor of a building facing the Hanuman Dhoka. The beautiful dining area fascinated me. We were seated on the floor (in a squatting position) on small cushions, and food was served on desk-like tables placed in front of the cushions. That brought back memories of my childhood; this was how we always had our meals in India. Food was served in copper dishes and I fell in love with the whole ambience. It had transferred me back in time, brought before my eyes the picture of old civilizations. From our dining area I could see the whole of the Square with all its shops, temples and all the activities on the streets. The young men who served us food were very hospitable with a charming smile. There are no words to describe Nepalese hospitality. One thing I am very certain is such a culture and hospitality have been nurtured and inherited for generations.

After lunch we visited the dreaded figure of Kal Bhairab (God of Destruction), coronation platform, statue of King Pratap Malla, Big Bell and drum. It also houses the renowned "Kumari Ghar" (the house of the Kumari or virgin or the living goddess), which was all located at Hanuman Dhoka. The whole square was lined with hundreds of handicrafts. Even I, never crazy about shopping, felt compelled to indulge a little. As for habitual shoppers, I am sure it is heaven on earth with the wide array of beautiful goods at reasonable prices.

On that evening i.e. May 8, 2003, Kumar joined us for dinner, and we finalized plans for the following day, as well as the whole trekking itinerary up to the Base Camp. The next morning I was to take the mountain flight. The local private airlines arrange flights up to Mount Everest. Those who do not trek to Everest take this flight. But the next day I could not take the mountain flight as it was cancelled, because of bad weather. We decided to take the mountain flight after my return from the MEBC.

During this trip to Everest Base Camp I also had an opportunity to travel by road around Nepal. The entire road trip was a journey by itself I visited Pokhra — the lake city, Lumbini, Chitwan Park, Janakpur and Highest resort in the Himalayan range.

Lumbini is the place Lord Buddha — the apostle of peace and the light of Asia was born in 623 B.C. This is the place which should be visited and seen by a person of devotion and should cause awareness and apprehension of the impermanence of life. As we entered the archaeologically restored palace, a feeling of serenity took over. Recently a group of archaeologists have been successful in relocating the marker stone placed by Emperor Ashoka to identify the exact place where Prince Siddhartha (Buddha) took his first step immediately after his birth in Lumbini. This area is well protected with a glass barrier. The visit to Lumbini left me with a feeling of great solace.

CHITWAN PARK EXPERIENCE

Chitwan is one of the few remaining undisturbed vestiges of the 'Terai' region, which formerly extended over the foothills of India and Nepal. It is a 937 Square-Kilometer preserve. It has a particularly rich flora and fauna. One of the last populations of single-horned Asiatic rhinoceros lives in the park, which is also one of the last refugees of the Bengal tiger. We reached Chitwan Park around 5 pm. It was too late to take the evening elephant ride, we decided to relax that evening. Around 6:30 pm we watched a documentary movie about the park. After dinner an interesting event was waiting for us.

After dinner we were escorted to an observation deck built over the riverbed. From this deck one can watch the animals that come to drink water in the river. On the deck I had opportunity to meet many families from the US and Australia. I also met a man from the US who had been to Mt. Everest Summit in 1993. The sunset changed the whole scenario of the forest — the chirping of countless birds, the myriad calls of wild animals. The fauna springs to life after the sun goes down. We did not happen to see any tigers or cheetah, but we did see lots of deer, wild pigs and buffaloes. There seemed to be a great rejoice among the trees and all fauna which had made this place their home. They existed for each other and above them was heaven — the God made. I could feel life, which was vast and splendid spreading in all directions. Life was there in abundance. After this wonderful experience we returned to our respective rooms. The rooms were wooden cabins with no electricity and minimal water supply. We were requested not to go alone outside the lodge compound and always be within the paved path. It was one of a kind experience. That night when I went to bed, I could hear lots of wild noises from the forest around.

The next day we rose early and headed for Elephant Safari. As I walked towards the platform, I could sense that someone was staring at me. I looked around to find a pair of beautiful eyes staring at me. I was stunned for a moment, looked into the eyes, which were gazing at me. I could feel a flash when our eyes met. When I smiled, it was immediately reciprocated.

When I was still mesmerized by the eyes, Raj broke my trance. He wanted me to move towards the raised platform where we mount the elephant's back. There was a box like seat on elephant's back and each box had room for four people and the mahout, the Elephant trainer. I mounted the elephants then again looked at the eyes, which were still looking at me. We exchanged the message that we can meet each other later after the Elephant Safari. The elephant took us into the wild dense forest. We had an opportunity to watch many animals and especially the single horned Rhinoceros, We returned to the platform around 8 am. While I was walking back into the lodge, I could not resist the feeling to search for the eyes, which had captivated me. To my surprise the beautiful eyes too were searching for me. After exchanging smiles with my new friend I moved into the lodge to have my breakfast.

After breakfast we set out for our Jungle walk of about 4 miles after getting lots of instruction from the guide. At the end of the walk we came to the other edge of the island. There were boats, which were ready to take us back to the lodge. The boat ride back to the lodge was smooth. When we reached the lodge, there was time to spare before lunch. The manager said that all elephants would be taken to the river for a bath and volunteers are welcome to help the elephant bathe. There were two teenage girls from Mexico who had wanted to volunteer and their mother was in a dilemma. When she knew I was going to volunteer, she wanted me to take care of her children. All the volunteers were taken to the river. There were six elephants, two of the volunteers were asked to mount each elephant. After we mounted the elephants, the mahout (elephant trainer) led all the elephants to the river. The elephants walked in to deeper waters and we remained on the back of the elephants. The Mahout instructed us on how to wash the elephants. Later the elephants walked to the shallow end of the river. They were able to lie down so that they can be washed. Still the two beautiful eyes were following every one of my act. My eyes fell on this great creation with the most beautiful and captivating eyes, struggling to scratch her back. I could not resist the urge to rush over and help her. There was a feeling of contentment in those beautiful eyes.

The local guide told me that the beautiful eyes were of Saraswathi ('Sara's'). She was brought into this island when she was 6 years old. No one knew where she came from and who her parents were. She was thirty-two years of age and she had lived in the island all the time. We had developed a strong bond and many people who had known Sara's were surprised. It was a great ego-booster to me that I could soon establish a relationship with this dame.

After the bathing ceremony, I silently bid goodbye to Sara's and returned to my room reluctantly. The bondage, which had developed between Sara's and me, was that of harmony. If two creations of God can establish an unconditional bondage by just communicating in silence, it is very surprising that we humans who have the ability of expressing ourselves by communicating to each other verbally fail to establish a loving bond with no expectations. It was time to leave Chitwan Park the next day; I could not help looking for Sara's. I did find the beautiful eyes staring back at me from behind a tree. Those beautiful eyes belonged to none but elegant elephant called Saraswathi (Sara's). We parted with a sweet and silent smile.

(Saras) – Chitwan National Park

FINAL PREPARATIONS

On May 9. 2003, I was to take the flight to Lukla, the starting point of the Mount Everest Base Camp (MEBC). The trek would be of 21 days to go to the Base Camp and return. I had no idea how these three weeks were going to be, except that I would need to keep walking and walking. Kumar had selected the best guide. It was Inder Narayan Rai, who was very familiar with all the routes, and spoke good English. In addition I also had services of a healthy youngster as my Sherpa, one who carried the luggage. Kumar made sure that I was fully equipped for the trek—trekking boots, warm clothing, emergency medicines, a sleeping bag and all gears needed for the trek.

I had brought two cameras from America. I knew this was a journey of a lifetime and did not want to lose any picture in the event I lost or damaged my camera. I also kept the two cameras in different bags, thinking that if I lost one, I would have the second camera as a backup. I was not an experienced photographer, and I had a standard automatic camera. As I did not know the gravity of this trip, it never occurred to me that I should have a movie camera, a Handy cam. Kumar and Raj helped me in packing all the things in order before bidding me good night with the instruction that we were to be at the airport by 6 am the next morning. The route of the trek was from Lukla at a height of 9253 feet to the North Ridge of Mount Everest Base Camp (MEBC) at a height of 18640 feet. As per the itinerary, the trek would take 21 days to complete. Trekking agency had made all arrangements for our trekking party to stay at the lodges on the way. Generally, they are family homes converted into lodges. They have main sitting areas with central heating and small rooms to sleep in. These lodges were located in small villages or towns depending on the population. Starting from Lukla. I stayed in the following lodges during my trek Jorsale, Namche Bazaar, Tengbuche, Periche, Lebuche, Gorak Shep, and the Mount Everest Base Camp. A village may have anywhere from ten houses to forty or fifty. In addition, a town would constitute hundreds of houses at these altitudes.

Before describing the trek, I want to talk about the Himalayan range. The Himalayan range runs a distance of two thousand kilometers from east of India to the west. The Himalayan range has the ten tallest peaks in the world. Eight of them are in Nepal with Mount Everest being the tallest of them, at a height of 8850 meters (29035 feet). All these peaks have base camps. Base camps are at the foothill of each mountain, used as a base for climbers. I was going to the Base Camp of Mount Everest.

FLIGHT TO LUKLA

On May 9, 2003, I rose at four and was ready by 5:45 am. Kumar and Raj accompanied by Indra Narayan Rai, my trekking guide, came to the hotel to pick me up. I found Inder to be a very cheerful person with a friendly smile. During the entire trek I never saw the smile leave him, except for one moment when a big boulder fell right in front of us. When we entered the lobby of the Katmandu airport, I saw hundreds of young men and women, with all the trekking gear, ready to fly lo Lukla. I was flabbergasted. So many of them, all bound to Mount Everest Base Camp? Is this a Jathra [Fair]? Unable to conceal my surprise, I asked Kumar if this was a regular sight. He smiled and said, "The year 2003 is the 50th year of reaching the peak Mount Everest and there are big celebrations going on and that is the reason trekkers, climbers, and tourists from all over the world are here. Sir Edmond Hillary will be here too for the celebrations." Until that moment, I was not aware of anything about the special event or the celebrations. It was a coincidence that I had chosen this time for my pilgrimage!

As I was ready to go through the security check, I noticed a concern in both Kumar and Raj's eyes. They must have been wondering, about what my fate was going to be with my age and my cardiac condition. Most of the fellow human beings with cardiac problems tend to think that it is the end of most of the activities and that he or she has come to the end of life's journey. Therefore, I was not surprised at their concern. However, they quickly hid their concern behind their pleasant smile and wished me good luck with a warm hug.

While waiting for the flight to Lukla in the security lobby, Inder and I took this opportunity to get to know each other better. Inder was a 28 year old young man with lots of grit and drive. He was married and he was a father of a little girl. He had been a trekking guide for the past eight years and was well aware of all the Himalayan passes in the vicinity. His

40

English was very fluent, as he had earned a graduate degree. I also shared some brief details about myself, my life and my family, when I mentioned the fact that I was recently promoted to the status of a grandfather, Inder said that I did not look my age. He also could not believe the fact that a person with my physique had undergone quadruple bypass!

We boarded a twin-engine propeller plane, which seats about fifty. As the plane ascended, I had a bird's eye view of Katmandu. I was amazed to see the amount of terrace farming done to grow paddy. I guessed that with such extensive cultivation and harnessing of the Himalayan waters, Nepal would be exporting rice. Later, I learnt that Nepal has to import rice to meet its own requirements as rice is the staple food of Nepalese.

As we headed towards Lukla, the Himalayan Range was to my left. I had a great view as I had an opportunity to sit on the left side behind the cockpit. At the very first glimpse I was awestruck by the majestic Himalayas. I was unable to comprehend the sky-reaching heights of the peaks. As each peak grew nearer I couldn't help wondering at the size of them. This kind of unspoken competition goes from peak to peak. I was filled with a calm, serene, and beautiful feeling.

After 40 minutes by air, there was a change in the direction of the flight, and I knew we were getting ready to land. As I was sitting behind the pilot, I could see every change in direction and altitude that was happening. I craned my neck 180 degrees to see where the landing strip was. Out of nowhere, right in front of us, there appeared a tiny runway, which inclined about 30 to 35 degrees. The sight of the little runway did get my adrenalin pumping. Landing the aircraft in such treacherous terrain demands great skill on the part of the pilot and more so, because of the sudden change of wind direction. We landed at Lukla, which is at the base of Khumbu region.

The feeling and the touch of the land of Himalayas put me in a different world. It was such a pleasant feeling of breathing the fresh air at that altitude of 9253 feet, even with atmospheric oxygen of 73%. I just stood and took a deep breath, enjoyed the feel of every molecule of air that went into my lungs. This is the purest natural form of oxygen I had ever breathed.

Inder, the guide took care of the formalities of security and baggage check. We met Pankaj, who was my Sherpa, the guy who carries the luggage. Sherpa are mostly local people; they have a way of carrying the luggage with ease, and walk with comfort in the rough terrain of the Himalayas. They carry most of the weight on the back of their spine. From the bottom end of the baggage. a ribbon-like hand takes the weight of the bag, and the top end of the band is fastened to the forehead. This makes the weight to distribute all the way from the forehead to the lower end of the spine. This keeps both hands free from holding the baggage. The Sherpas are generally youngsters but you can find some elderly people doing this job for a living.

START OF
THE TREK

FIRST DAY - TREK TO JORSALE

We began our trek from Lukla with our small backpacks. The weather was hot and humid. I wore trekking trousers and a full sleeve shirt for the first day's trek. Inder had already decided that Phakding, at a height of 2623 meters (8655 feet) would be our next stop, a descent of 900 feet. Descending towards Phakding the very first mountain edge I came across was so overwhelming. It was almost touching the sky. On the other side, the valley went so deep down that I felt like it was touching the bottom of the earth. Walking on the mountains surrounded by valleys, there was complete solitude. The beauty of the mountains and the solitude it provided was beyond thought and feeling. The solitude was not static or still, it was living and moving. I was drowned in the solitude provided by these great mountain ranges.

At the next turn, the next peak and the valley made the previous ones pale in comparison in terms of both size and breath taking image. Now I remembered the statement made by the Internet chat friend who said, "Take a thousand Rocky Mountains, and put them in one place and it will make a part of Himalayas." How true it was. On reaching Phakding in 4 hours, we were met by our Sherpa Pankaj who was carrying our baggage. Having walked for 4 hours, we were famished. In Phakding, we had lunch, which consisted of vegetable soup, Nepali roti (flatbread), rice, curry and plenty of vegetables.

After lunch Inder asked me if I wanted to continue the trek or stay at Phakding for that night. As I was not tired and the time was still 1 p.m. not wanting to waste precious hours, I wanted to continue the trek towards Jorsale at (9900 feet, Oxygen 65%). Expected trekking time was around four to five hours. We continued our trek towards Jorsale from Phakding at a brisk pace.

During this leg of the trek, I met a nice gentleman, Craig Malouf, from Sydney, Australia. As we walked from Phakding to Jorsale we found so many things to talk about and share. I was amazed to notice how much we had in common, whether it was appreciating Mother Nature or pondering about Life back in cities. Malouf was a retired football player from Australia with a love for world travel. I learned a lot from him, about all the places he had visited and his experiences. Our meeting made me feel as if all men from distant corners of the world could carry the same thoughts and feelings, "Why can't we all live in harmony, in this beautiful world?" When I met Mr. Craig Malouf, it was just the beginning of my trek. There was so much to absorb, understand, learn, and see—the realities of life through the heart.

We reached Jorsale at 4:30 p.m. It was not an easy trek given the ascent of 1245 feet. I was tired after eight hours of trekking; we decided to stay for the night at Jorsale. As I was hungry, we had our dinner and I was in bed by 5 p.m. Though I was tired there was no obvious discomfort or cause for any concern given the cardiac condition as the heart rate was within the normal range. Respiration was normal—no hyper-ventilation or panting. There was no headache or nausea. I drowned into deep sleep wondering what was waiting for tomorrow.

Lama Script on the Rock – 9ᵗʰ May 2003.

DAY TWO - TREK TO
NAMCHE BAZAAR

The next day, May 10, 2003, we left Jorsale at 7 a.m. after breakfast to Namche Bazaar (10,662 feet, oxygen 66%) at around 3 p.m. The temperature was cooler than the previous day with sun shining bright and I wore a sweater to keep warm. It was uphill all the way. There was a little thinning of the air but there was no shortness of breath, no chest discomfort, and there was no body pain. As we continued our trek, my walk was getting slower, I started talking less, became more introspective and lost myself in the serenity of the mountains.

Whenever I saw a village or a hamlet on the way, I could not help but wonder, "What prompted these people to live at these heights? What an amount of hardship they had to face every day?" Is it the spirituality of the place? On the other hand, is it to get away from the artificiality of city life? Then these people might wonder what compelled the urbanites to live in congested, air-polluted, noise-polluted, light-polluted, cri me-ridden concrete jungles, just for the necessities of life? May be we are leading a life untrue to our nature by living in big urban areas. Otherwise why would we possess time shares in country resorts on an island, near a lake or on the mountains?

Though I was getting tired, the body was functioning in the normal range. Due to low oxygen and reduced atmospheric pressure, my fingers swelled. I would every once in a while raise my hands above my head and clenched fists, to decrease the swelling. I noticed that other young trekkers did not develop this symptom. I thought the age factor and cardiac conditions might have triggered the swelling. I observed that my thinking process was also getting lethargic. This was probably due to tiredness, coupled with oxygen deficiency. During the trek I met other trekkers from Germany, New Zealand, Denmark, England and the USA.

Namche Bazaar is a beautiful town. The view from every lodge here is the same. The whole town appeared picturesque. The buildings were colorful, and narrow roads wound from one end of the town to the other. We reached Namche Bazaar around 3 p.m. After checking into a lodge we visited Sir Edmund Hilary Museum and then went to the fair. It was the shanty (weekly market) day in Namche Bazaar. The hill people had gathered from all over to sell, buy, and swap goods such as clothing, food grains vegetables, eggs, meat, oil, fruits, goats, chicken, sheep, yaks, and utensils. It was quite a sight to watch life bubbling like that and suddenly coming to an end by the evening.

Overall I went to bed that day feeling a little exhausted because of the trekking and the change in altitude. My heart rate, respiration and mental status were all normal with no major changes.

Namche Bazar.

Mr. Gumbu Sherpa - First Indian to reach Mt. Everest Summit
Mr. Jim Whittaker (First American to reach Mt. Everest Summit

First Step at MEBC.

<Insert Base Camp May 16ᵗʰ here >
With Inder (Guide) and Pankaj (Sherpa)

Chief Coordinator – Mt. Everest Marathon Committee 2003.

Mr. Lokendra Bahadur Chand- Prime Minister Nepal – 2003.

With Mr. Reinhold Messner -Reached Mt. Everest Summit without Extra Oxygen.

DAY THREE - TREK TO TENGBUCHE

The next morning, May 11, 2003, after breakfast we left Namche Bazaar enroute to Tengbuche. My physical condition was normal in all aspects Inder told me that the Tengbuche monastery was one of the oldest and largest in that region. The trekking path became steeper and more rugged. As the trek became strenuous, I grew tired. At every step and turn, the view became more and more gorgeous. Whenever I was too tired to move, I would stand by and stare at the mountains, trying to figure out what magnetic power these mountains possess to be pulling people from all over the world.

I had heard that once a person goes trekking in the mountains, he is hooked. This I never understood before. In the first place, I had never figured out why people went on treks at all. I always thought it was just walking aimlessly. Though I had a flair for other adventurous things like sky diving, scuba diving, and white-water rafting, trekking never interested me. How wrong I was. I realized that the mountains had let me find out the truth myself. A shudder went through my body. I apologized to them, and was ready to receive anything that came my way to learn.

By noon we found a lodge and had our lunch. Now my body was demanding three square meals a day. Continuing our journey, we reached Tengbuche at about 2 p.m. and refreshed ourselves by having a delightful cup of hot lemon tea. Our lodge was opposite the Tengbuche monastery. At 4 p.m. there was prayer service at the monastery, which I wanted to attend. As there was some time left for the service. I decided to visit the local museum. In the museum there were other trekkers. It contained the photographs of many great mountaineers, samples of local arts and crafts, books, and souvenirs. They had a small projection room, where a documentary film on Tengbuche Monastery was shown. I saw a movie of the Tengbuche festival, inaugurated by Sir Edmond Hillary. The prayer and chanting on the occasion, accompanied by drums, bells and flute, were so vibrant that I was mesmerized. I wondered: "If this is my experience sitting in this small auditorium and watching it, what will the real experience be?"

The Tengbuche Monastery is one of the largest and oldest monasteries in the Himalayas. Sitting on a hill peak, it is a superb structure with a magnificent view. Many monks and student recruits lived in the monastery. As you enter the hall you see a huge (about 12 feet tall), wooden statue of Gautama Buddha. Being a Soumya Murthy (Serene Buddha), he does not awe you, but with a tinge of smile on his face he seems to lovingly welcome you into his presence. I have seen several statues of Buddha in different parts of the world; this statue of Buddha had a tinge of serene smile that made it look different from other statues I had come across.

At the stroke of 4 p.m. the chanting began to the accompaniment of the drums and bells. The vibrations penetrate the heart, and the entire body started Pulsating. I felt as if I were entering a different plane on this earth. After some time the music alternated from chanting to drums, bells, and then a combination of all. You cannot become anything but mesmerized by the happenings. The novices take active part in chanting and playing the drums and bells. There is an order to who should lead and who should follow. The Senior Monk starts the chanting and the youngest student concludes the chant. They observe the same hierarchy in the beating of the drums and bells and singing of songs.

After reaching a crescendo, the prayer came to a stop with a big bang, exactly at 5 p.m. In a very orderly fashion the Lama students prostrate themselves before the Soumya Murthy (Serene Buddha) and walk out. As they leave, they do not turn their backs to the deity. Instead, they walk backwards step by step until they reach the exit. The whole ceremony left me wondering about the richness of this heritage and culture. Their discipline and dedication impressed me. On the other hand it would be difficult to miss the perpetual serene smile on the faces of these holy men. The smile was a welcoming smile for me. The smile passed into me the peaceful thoughts of these holy men.

The smile radiated from the Monks also made me conclude human beings can find peace and happiness within themselves as their attachment to material pleasures reduces. When I was practicing as a doctor, I conducted lectures on the topic "Philosophy of Mental Relaxation". In these workshops I usually emphasized the fact "Less is more, and more is less," and, "Everything is nothing. and nothing is everything", I am not against material success but we should set our limits on how far we can push ourselves in this pursuit to the extent we are not to be possessed by materialistic things.

As we walked out of the monastery, a thick wafer of cloud drifted slowly at our eye level. As we watched, it covered a group of people standing nearby. The lower half of their bodies became invisible for some time as the cloud covered them, and then slowly moving away. The cloud was like a flame with the light of the setting sun; no fantasy could build such a cloud. No architect could have designed such a structure. It was the result of many winds, sun, pressures and strains. Experiencing such a beautiful cloud over the mountains with no thoughts was like a miracle. While I was mesmerized with these intense clouds for ten minutes, the first layer of cloud had passed by, and another layer of clouds came in. This time it covered just the upper half of the bodies of those standing there, and exposed only the lower part. Until time for dinner at 6:30 p.m. I spent the time in solitude savoring the beauty of Mother Nature. The experience of being in absolute nothingness was so blissful.

Over dinner we discussed the next day's itinerary and agreed to leave about 7 am in the morning, after breakfast. I was more exhausted than the previous night. I noticed that my heart rate and respiration which had increased during the end of that day's trekking, were normal at bed time.

DAY FOUR-TREK TO PERICHE

As soon as I woke up at six in the morning on May 12, 2003, I felt unclean and desperately wanted to shower. It was four days since I had a shower though I was accustomed to showering in the morning and evening. I told the lodge owner that I'd like to take a shower. It may amuse the readers as to why on earth I had to tell the owner of the lodge about wanting to have a shower. Well, the bathroom was outside the building where the lodge is located. On the second floor of the lodge we have a large bucket into which hot almost boiling water is poured. But by the time it reaches the bathroom (wooden enclosure), which is 25 feet away, by a rubber pipe, fitted with a shower-head, the water turns cold. When I informed the manager that I was ready in the bathroom, he filled the bucket with hot water, which turned cold by the time it reached the bath area on the ground floor. As I was used to ice cold showers at home, I could handle this.

After taking a quick shower, I wrapped myself in a towel, and ran to the room to dress for the day but trouble started. Even after dressing, my feet were still freezing cold. It felt as if pins and needles were stuck in them. I put on socks and boots. Still the burning pain in the toes was there. I was scared that I was encountering frostbite. I spot jumped to restore circulation. I felt better. Then I realized my mistake. I was forgetting that the whole place, including my room, bathroom, and the yard was ice cold.

And so was everything that I touched. I put on my clothes, socks, shoes, the overcoat (used in trekking) and gloves! Still shivering, I remembered that the only warm place was the dining hall. I ran into the hall and cuddled up before the hearth. I sat there until I felt warm and comfortable. Later when I told Inder about the incident, he was not amused. He admonished me to check with him first before I attempted anything like that again.

At this point of time a flash of thought went through my mind. If only we humans could take a shower with the water of honesty, purity, simplicity, forgiveness, charity, and love which would clean the sweat and dirt of hatred, jealousy, revenge, and hypocrisy from our hearts, the world would become a peaceful place. The world needs this Spiritual Internal cleansing to make it a better place to live.

After breakfast we left Tengbuche and started towards Periche. Tengbuche was behind us now (altitude 12893 feet, oxygen 62%). and we were headed for Periche (15157 feet and 55% respectively). It meant a huge difference of almost 3000 feet and a diminished oxygen saturation of 8%. I was not sure what was to come, or how my body would react to this change in altitude. It was a long trek.

During the trek towards Periche I met two gentlemen who were elderly and looked at least seventy returning from the Base camp. One of them was Mr. Jim Whittaker an American and the other Mr. Gambu Sharpa an Indian. They both were the first to scale Mount Everest for their respective countries back in 1963. They had trekked to MEBC to celebrate the 50th Anniversary of conquering Mount Everest. I was amazed that they were game to trek to MEBC despite their age and they were in turn amazed to know that I was attempting to get to MEBC despite the quadruple bypass. I took pictures with these legends. They wished me the best and had a parting word of advice "Pay due respect to the altitude, and try to play it safe at every step."

After the chance encounter with the legends the trek continued. Physically I was doing all right. There were no obvious signs to worry. I noticed that I was urinating more than usual. Does it have something to do with my consuming more fluids, or the high altitude? I did not know. And I also was experiencing flatulence. Perhaps it was due to the change of diet, I thought. Later, I found out that it was a normal phenomenon. It is called High Altitude Flatulence (HAF), and was due to decreased air pressure. As the atmospheric pressure decreases, the gas within expands. As the gas expands, there will be abdominal bloating.

We encountered more bridges across small streams or rivulets than before. Most of them were wooden suspension bridges, and many were being upgraded into metal and cable bridges. The first one we came across was a really old, dilapidated wooden bridge, its looks really concerned me, conquered my initial apprehensions and proceeded further, and later during the trek came across many such bridges. I remembered the saying, which I had read long time back, "Every day we are given stones. But you must decide whether to build a bridge or a wall". If only we can learn to build bridges of love and compassion, cross the ravines of hatred, jealousy and vengeance, there would be no resistance or barriers inwardly towards anything. The world would be free from conflicts and hypocrisies, we can feel the beauty of love inside and outside, everywhere in the world.

At the next turn of the pass. I suddenly saw a mountain of a different kind. This mountain was made up of brown rocks. My eyes scanned it from the base to the top. At the peak of the mountain, in the midst of these rocks, is a large, beautiful tree all-alone. In its solitude it dominated the whole mountain. I admired it with its large trunk deeply embedded in the earth, solid and indestructible, its branches long, dark and spread. At sight of the tree several questions flashed into my mind. How powerful was the supernatural power of God that took the seed to that altitude? The immense love of Mother Nature, which tendered and nurtured the seed into a plant. What supernatural strength of a Father, who had protected this plant and turned it into a magnificent tree? What supernatural harmony of Mother Nature, which kept the tree on top of the mountains amidst these rocks and boulders? The answer lies in the heart, soul and eye of the beholder.

We continued our walk silently. Walking in the deep shadows of a mountain I felt a deep silence conquering me. I felt vulnerable and very open, "I" hardly seemed to exist. The beauty of the mountain was greatly moving. My feet were doing their job of carrying me safely. At every step they were cautious to see that no harm came to me. Suddenly I realized what a beautiful mode of transportation feet are. They make sure that the body is in the right place, in the right location, keeping perfect balance, giving me as little shock as possible. We take our feet for granted and never appreciate their worth. My brain and my feet were doing such good team work. At times when my feet wanted to land in a certain location, my brain, like a charioteer guiding the horse, would advise my feet to change the location of landing so as to keep the balance and safety of my body.

As I continued to walk. I accidentally stumbled on a piece of rock, balancing myself I kicked a small pebble that rolled about ten to fifteen feet ahead of me. For some reason or another I bent down, picked up the pebble felt sorry for kicking it. I felt that I had disturbed the harmony of the pebble. The pebble was trying to convey many things to me. I tried to look around the mountains: there I found a large boulder delicately balanced on the edge of the mountain. The boulder appeared to be on the verge of rolling down. On the base of the boulder I found a small pebble similar to the one I had in my hand. For an onlooker the pebble seems to be balancing the entire boulder.

I was awestruck at the "Harmony of Nature in Life". The rocks, pebbles, the boulders of the mountains were so alive, they all seemed to run after the clouds. The clouds clung to them, taking the shapes of the rocks and pebbles they flowed around them. Suddenly I could feel the rocks around me they were gentle and of so many shapes and sizes. They were so indifferent to everything, to the rains, to the winds and the disturbances caused by men. They had been there and will continue to be there. As I walked along the mountains, everything seemed to be close and delicate. All this extravagant beauty, this rich Mother Earth, the great Himalayas, all these were within one. With the heart and the brain completely open, without the barrier of time and space, there was only this beauty, without sound and form. Everything else ceased, only Himalayas existed.

We stopped in a wayside hotel to have some lemon tea. I met Lisa and Linda, medical students, and Chuck, a registered nurse, all from America. After becoming better acquainted, I requested that they check my pulse. Considering that they were young, we took their pulse rate as normal, given the conditions of exhaustion and lack of oxygen. But we were all surprised to see that while my pulse rate was between 90 and 110, and that of these youngsters ranged from 100 to 120. We continued our trek. I met more trekkers whose pulse rate was higher than mine, this despite the age and cardiac condition I told them that I had been meditating for over ten years and it had helped me in controlling both my heart rate and respiration. During the trek, whenever I felt tired, which meant my heart rate was not under control, I would stop walking, and find a comfortable place to go into meditation until my heart rate returned to normal. My guide Inder and Sherpa Pankaj were intrigued by this in the beginning but later they could guess exactly when I was going to stop for meditation.

The higher we went, thinner the air became and I depended on meditations to keep progressing. I also noticed my breathing was normal whenever I was passing a 'Green belt'. Mother Nature provided a harmony by creating trees, which provide Oxygen for human beings, but we destroy trees and ignore the fact that man is part of this environment and nature. Man had destroyed trees to build cities and factories. By this action human beings are cut off from Nature. Man-made buildings have taken the place of forests and valleys. Today we have to buy fresh and purified water as we have polluted our eco system. Currently we have also formed concepts of Oxygen bars where one pays to get some pure oxygen to breathe. It is time we realized the fact that we have to live with nature and not destroy it further.

At this point I was reminded of an event that happened when I went for white-water rafting (WWR) in the Colorado River, Grand Canyon. It was a full day's event; from 6 am to 6 p.m. We were picked up at 4 am from the hotel and driven to the river. The raft organizers were all Native American Indians. The captain of our group, also a native, clearly instructed us not to touch the river water without his approval. He was very firm about this. We vacated the van at the bank of the Colorado River, deep in the Grand Canyon. We were at a depth of one mile below the normal ground level. He made all of us stand in a line about ten feet from the river. He went closer to the water and offered prayers in his American Indian way to the River. Reverently kneeling down, with both hands he picked up the water and sprinkled it on his head. With his second handful of water he sprinkled it on all of us. Later he turned around and explained to us what his prayer signified. He had requested the River to be like our mother and protect us like her children. For during the rafting we would be jumping and stamping all over her body like a child who jumps all over its mother. As the mother who would enjoy such play of her children, so would the River treat us and protect us. Only after taking the mother River Colorado's permission he said, could we put our feet in the water. He made each one of us stand close to the water, asked us to pray in our own language to any God we believed in. We were told to take the water in both hands and take the permission of the River and sprinkle the water on our heads. Only after doing this were we allowed to place our feet into the water. We realized the value of this prayer when the fury of the Colorado became apparent within five minutes.

At the start, we had a smooth float on the river, but within minutes our rafts were going on a roller coaster ride, with straight drops of fifteen to twenty feet! We were tossed from one end to the other. It was like brushing with death at every turn of the river. No wonder we needed the tender care and protection of the mother. Our group leader continued to tell us to treat the Mother Earth with tender love and affection. He mentioned that for the native Indians made sure that they never left a mark on the ground while moving to a different location from one camp to another. They would even fill in the holes of the pegs of tents with soil. They left Mother Earth the way they found her. This was a great experience wherein

I could realize that in our great rush to live our lives we completely ignore Nature and forget that we need to respect and honor Nature as we coexist.

With these thoughts, as trekking continued I was becoming very tired, as the path became more rugged, trees got fewer, and the air became thinner. Suddenly Inder asked me to take a look at the mountains in front of us. There was a landslide. I was shocked to see almost one quarter of the mountain slid into the valley and disappear into the boisterous flowing river. I could experience the scars of Mother Nature. Human beings have been ignoring Nature and keep destroying the gifts of Mother Nature. It is time we establish a deep, long abiding relationship with nature - with the trees, bushes, mountains, forests and the fast moving clouds — then this Universe would be a better place to live.

We reached Periche (15,157 feet and 55% oxygen) at about 4 p.m. I was exhausted due to the increase in altitude and lesser oxygen concentration. My heart rate was increasing more frequently than the previous days and also my respiration was rapid and shallow. We went straight to the lodge, had some snacks and a cup of hot lemon juice. With this my physical status came to normal range. We were told the village clinic, 'Trekkers Aid Post' run by the Himalayan Rescue Association, the last major medical center on the way to Everest, was at the other end of the village. It was about a quarter of a mile from the lodge. After resting for 30 minutes we went to the medical center.

At the medical center I met Dr. Kristen, who was in-charge of the Center. She was surprised that despite the cardiac conditions I had undertaken the trek. She mentioned that she had heard about four years ago a European had attempted to go to the Base Camp but he gave up half way and returned. Dr. Kristen had some advice for the next leg of the trek. She mentioned that danger lay in 'Not respecting the altitude'. That caused people to end up with altitude sickness and may even cause death. She warned that from now on the air would become thinner, the grade of uphill steeper and the path more rugged. She advised that consumption of lot of fluids (water) was important. She recommended that I stop at the next station, which was Dugla. Though the trekking distance to Dugla from Periche was only two hours, it would be best according to her to stay there overnight to get acclimatized to the altitude, and then proceed further. Lebuche, the next station was at least 5 hours of trekking away from Dugla with Altitude of 16853 and oxygen saturation of 53%. To proceed straight to Lebuche would be a huge strain on the body. She then did a general physical examination. My pulse, blood pressure, respiration and heart rare were all within the normal range.

I went back to the lodge after thanking Dr. Kristen, went to bed with thoughts about the onward trek and the challenges it may pose. At the end of the night when I retired, I was comfortable with my vital signs but was feeling exhausted.

DAY FIVE - TREK TO LEBUCHE

Day of Foolhardy Decision

I woke up at six in the morning on May 13, 2003, after breakfast left Periche at 7 am. Passed the medical center on the way and remembered the warning of Dr. Kristen 'Respect the altitude and be careful at every step from now on". Directly in front of the clinic there is a memorial listing all the names of the people who have died on Everest. The structure resembles a mountain (cone) cut into half and spread apart. The gap in between these two halves is just enough for a person to walk through. Climbers walk between the two separated cones as a mark of respect. The message of the monument is that, you may get in and come out of this gap successfully, and if someone fails to return from the trek, his or her name would be etched for posterity.

After paying homage to the departed souls we headed towards Dugla, it was necessary to pass through a valley. During monsoon this dry valley would be a boisterous stream. Now the riverbed was marshy and amid puddles of water were plenty of rocks and small boulders. We had to tread on these rocks carefully as they were smooth and slippery. A couple of times I did slip and land in the marsh but fortunately did not twist or sprain my ankles. The rocks had formed a natural bridge for the trekkers to cross to the other side during summer. The rest of the time they would be submerged under water. These rocks reminded me of the great human beings in real life, who rise up in the times of need to provide unselfish service for humanity and then return to their seclusion.

Monument for those who parted in this Adventure.

We crossed the marshy valley to reach the other side of the ravine. The stream, joined by other little streams rambled through the valley. It had its own moods but was always pleasant. They came down through different valleys and originated from different sources. They all joined the bigger stream, which was wider and deeper. It was a very soothing experience watching the streams and listening to their chatter. Wooden or stone bridges crossed these large streams. Crossing those bridges up in the mountains was quite a different thing. I could experience peace and complete silence within myself.

The trek continued towards Dugla. Looking beyond the mountains as I was walking, I noticed the houses and huts built using rocks and boulders. The craftsmanship of these people living on the mountains was amazing; they had used the rocks and boulders of different shapes to build a house. They lived amidst Mother Nature and they also used these sources available on the mountains to build their homes. We left the valley and started climbing the mountain. The terrain was becoming more rugged. We reached Dugla around 9.30 am. We stopped at a lodge and had a cup of hot lemon tea. Then we pondered over the fact whether we should stop at Dugla for the day or proceed further to our next stop Lebuche. Inder told me it would take 4 to 5 hours to reach Lebuche if we maintain the current pace.

Dugla was not at a high altitude and it did not offer a panoramic view. The place did not have many amenities. It was around 9:30 am and I was feeling energetic. Inder and Pankaj were also chirpy. With 4 to 5 hours of trek it would be only 3 p.m. to reach Lebuche and we would still have plenty of day time left. Considering the facts, I decided to proceed to Lebuche. In my enthusiasm I completely ignored Dr. Kristen's warning. **This was the first wrong decision I made on this trek**. My audacity won over my caution.

We headed towards Lebuche. The terrain became rough; we had hardly walked for thirty minutes when the climb became almost vertical. There was no track on the rugged rocks and no greenery anywhere in sight. I realized that I had made a wrong decision but kept walking. My heart was dancing for want of oxygen. As the physical strain increased, the heart rate increased, respiration also was rapid and shallow which made me light headed and my judgment was also becoming poor. After about an hour my physical body did not have much strength. At this point I realized it was time to exert my inner, spiritual strength rather than pushing my physical strength that was almost exhausted. I also debated on the fact whether I should go back to Dugla, get acclimatized to the altitude and then proceed to Lebuche. I shunned the idea of going back to Dugla.

There are people with different attitudes and temperaments: people who are logical in their acts; the other category that takes chances on calculated/healthy risks; and the final category whose actions have no logic or reasoning. At this juncture, I fitted in the final category and headed towards Lebuche. I did realize that I was not taking a logical or reasonable decision. It was a suicidal decision considering my cardiac problem.

Posted along the Trail.

The trek was becoming harder, the terrain rougher, the path steeper, and my heart rate was increasing by the minute. I was in no position to look around and enjoy nature. My primary concern was to keep my body in balance and carry it to the next lodging station. With the hope of finding a little oxygen, I started looking for trees and greenery. I even went in search of green bushes. Inder and Pankaj were initially surprised by my action. When I explained to them the process of photosynthesis they could appreciate my action. Oh God! How precious this oxygen is! How precious this life is!

I noticed my legs were getting tired and weak. I had not noticed this kind of weakness until now. My arm movements too became less frequent, and even to lift my arm was a task in itself. My heart rate was increasing; my respiration was becoming shallow and rapid. My walking became very slow. I started resting more and walking less. At this point Dr. Kristen's warning kept ringing in my mind. I started noticing the early signs of altitude sickness, such as severe headache, nausea, pulsations behind the eyeballs and palpitations, combined with the rapid and shallow respiration. Though the nausea was intense, fortunately I did not throw up during the entire trek.

Inder and Pankaj were very concerned watching me suffer. They could do nothing to decrease my plight except to offer sympathy and kind words. We all knew it was too late to go back to Dugla and we had to move forward to Lebuche as we had only an hour's trek remaining. Though going back to Dugla would be an easier trail, as it would have been downhill. I was determined to move towards the target even though I realized this part of the trek would take more than an hour considering my physical energy levels. At this point, Inder even took my backpack and relieved me of that extra load. We continued the trek. I was drinking lots of water and also munching the Snicker bars. All of us were tired and we continued our trekking with minimal conversation.

POWERS OF MEDITATION

Throughout my trek I took refuge with Meditation whenever I was in complete physical exhaustion. Meditation from my experience is not a means to an end. There is no end and no start. It is a movement in time and out of time. During meditation, thoughts and feelings flourish and die; it is a movement beyond time. These are the three things involved in meditation: relaxation, watching, and no judgement. Slowly a great silence descends over you. All movement within you ceases. There is no sense of "I am". Just a pure space. Meditation provides a sense of complete emptiness and ecstasy. Meditation had helped me find peace within myself when I had lost everything materially, self-discipline, imagination and peace of mind.

Whenever I stopped for resting, I sat in silence and went into the treasure of my inner strength as a source of spiritual energy. I went into deep meditation. It is amazing what a difference it made. An ounce of action is said to be better than a pound of words. In the similar manner I can say from experience 'An ounce of inner strength is greater than tons and tons of physical strength.' As I have been practicing meditation for the last fifteen years, and doing deep meditation for the past ten years, I have come to realize the power of meditation. Through meditation I have learned to harness the tremendous energy that we have within our own being. We do this by thinking focused and empowering thoughts. It's a practice by which I could calm the mind so that I can be nourished and strengthened by my own inner peace and stillness. I consider myself fortunate to realize the treasure of inner strength. Whenever my physical or mental strengths are tested, my inner strength has acted as my support system.

As we continued the trek, every step was harder than the previous one and every turn was difficult. It appeared that the mountains were testing my strength. The harder the trek progressed I too was adamant and determined to reach Lebuche, getting my strength from the same mountains. I was in La-La land due to the altitude effect, decreased oxygen and physical exhaustion. This resulted in increased heart rate, shallow and rapid breathing and uncertainty of thoughts.

My fatigue and heart rate were very high. The headache was increasing. I was becoming disoriented because of lack of oxygen; even the simple act of breathing was very difficult. But I kept progressing at a slow pace. At the turn of the next mountain, standing on a cliff, I saw a beautiful view of the mountain. It appeared in the shape of a human body. I could associate myself with it. The top of the mountain was my head, the mass was my trunk, the extensions were my arms and the base of the mountains was my legs. The trees, plants and shrubs were my nervous system streams running on the mountains were my blood; the wind that blew on the mountains was my breath; and I felt one with the mountains. This oneness with the mountains provided me with more inner strength, which gave me the encouragement to proceed with the trek.

Throughout the trek, Inder always walked a few yards ahead of me and I was followed by Pankaj. We kept walking with no exchange of words. At one point in time I felt a pat on my back. I presumed that Pankaj had wanted to say something and turned around. But he was a few yards away from me and he could not have touched me from that distance. I started to walk and again felt the pat on my back. Illusion? Probably but it was so real. I felt that the mountains were trying to tell me something. I tried to focus and everything became too intense. Spiritually I became 'one' with the mountains. When this oneness passed, my mental conversation with the mountains started. Mighty Mountains said as a fortunate pilgrim who had come up to this level, I needed to leave something behind and also take something with me from the mountains. I replied it would be my pleasure; I would leave behind my little anger and disturbed mind, take with me Absolute Peace and Eternal Bliss from the Great Mountains Listening to my response, Mountain said. "They are heavy. How are you going to leave them?" I responded saying that in the basket called 'Nirvana' (Complete Detachment) which had been bestowed on me by the Mighty Mountains.

The Mountains gave me a smile and asked me to continue progressing until I reach the goal.

Depending on the imagination of the reader, this experience of mine can be considered as hallucination or as being philosophical or having a spiritual out of body experience. But the fact is I did have this conversation with the Mountains.

There was a battle occurring between my physical strength and my inner strength. I was completely exhausted and in a hallucinatory state. I had one other interesting encounter with Death. I had been feeling his presence a short while after leaving Dugla when the terrain was getting rougher with less Oxygen around. Everything became intense and there was Death. Merely the brain was moving the leg that was all. I could feel Death. There was no deception or imagination; it was so much with me. I started to have a little conversation with Death. I told Death I was ready to go with him and wanted him to relieve me of this agony of living. For which he answered that it was not my time yet. This out of body conversation with DEATH made me realize that Death was always there, waiting and watching. No one can escape it and there is no necessity to be scared of DEATH. Life and Death are inseparable. Live the life, which has been bestowed on you; nothing is permanent, so 'let us live for the Day'.

After a couple of hours of trekking we were almost on top of one of the peaks. At this point, Inder said once we finish the climb, Lebuche is only a short distance. We only must go downhill from the top and cross a bridge. This information was of great relief for me. The altitude sickness was really making me tired and my legs had lost their strength. I was forced to stop every 5 to 10 steps to rest. I did not discuss with Inder and Pankaj about my plight. But they could deduce my plight from my face. Both of them were very helpful and took good care of me by providing water whenever I stopped despite them also being very tired and exhausted. With all my prayer and well wishes of Inder and Pankaj we reached the top of the peak, which was followed by a 30 minutes' walk on flat terrain to Lebuche. Even this flat terrain was extremely tiresome. As I was walking with my head down, suddenly Pankaj said "Papa, lift your head, you can see Lebuche. For some unknown reasons Pankaj suddenly started calling me Papa; I felt like my children were with me on the journey.

At 4:30 p.m. we reached Lebuche. We secured a room in the nearest lodge, ordered the menu for dinner. After having a cup of lemon tea at the dining hall, I went to my room, crashed on the bed without even removing off my trekking jacket. After about an hour Pankaj came to my room to announce that dinner was ready. Somehow I managed to go to the dining hall where I gulped my food and headed back to my room to go to bed.

That night I was too exhausted and tired. I still experienced the symptoms of Altitude Sickness-headache, nausea and dizziness. I shifted between deep sleep and semi-conscious sleep. Whenever I made an attempt to turn to a different position, I was confused. Even the smallest act of moving my hand woke me up as it required lots of energy and I was also hyper-ventilating (breathing rapidly). Later I learned that this was a common phenomenon with any novice trekker. The explanation, which I can provide as a doctor; is that every movement of the body demands oxygen. At higher altitude like this there is less availability of Oxygen. As a result we were forced to hyper-ventilate. It was one of the nights I did not know what was happening. There was no thinking, no orientation, no reasoning and no judgment.

DAY SIX - REST, CONTEMPLATION AND HARD DECISIONS

The next morning i.e. May 14, 2003 when I awoke there was an intense headache and fatigue. I realized that I was still under the spell of altitude sickness and had no idea how long those symptoms would last. All that I knew was that I have to relax and rest until all the symptoms are gone before I progress further on the trek. After the foolhardy decision of the previous day, I could completely understand the warning of Dr. Kristen of 'Respecting the Altitude'.

After breakfast and a hot cup of lemon tea around 8 am, I requested Inder and Pankaj to wake me at 1 p.m. just before having lunch. I went back to my room and started sleeping. I was too tired even to sit. It was so cold that day that I had to wear my jacket while sleeping. The room, where I was staying, had no heat and it was just an 8 ft. by 6 ft. plywood structure. I did not even have the stamina to change position while sleeping as that would result in hyper-ventilation. I tried to sleep. I was once again drifting between sleep and a semi-conscious state.

Thinking about that situation now makes me smile but it was definitely not a laughing matter at that time. This situation made me realize how God has provided us with everything but we do not appreciate the things provided. Though I had a near death experience a few years ago when I had the head injury, this experience of breathing in a reduced level of oxygen made me realize that we human beings take our lives for granted. As I was drifting into sleep, Inder came to announce that it was time for lunch. Reluctantly I sat up, freshened up and started towards the dining hall. While we were walking to the dining room Inder wanted to know whether I wanted to proceed to Gorak Shep that afternoon. I told him, as I was still suffering from altitude sickness, we would stay tonight. I could see a sigh of relief on the face of Inder.

The lodge where we were staying was family owned and operated. There was an old fireplace in the middle of the hail, where they used dried dung, wood, paper and anything that could burn to make a fire. Everyone huddled around the fireplace to stay warm. Attached to the dining hall/lounge was the kitchen. This place was not a sophisticated lodge. There were other trekkers in the dining area and we began sharing our trekking experience. Most of them were young and they too had undergone the same trauma which I experienced.

After lunch I went to my room and went to sleep again. My body was so exhausted it needed all the sleep and rest for recuperation and acclimatization. Being a doctor myself, I realized the risk of harming my heart (which was already damaged) further, that a place like this could be even more dangerous. At this time I did not even think about the plans for tomorrow. Once again Inder and Pankaj woke me for a cup of tea. They had made all arrangements for me to brush and freshen up before waking me up. I was touched by their friendly gesture. After having some snacks and a hot cup of tea I felt better. My headache and exhaustion had subsided, my heart rate and breathing were close to normal and I was getting acclimatized. Inder too noticed the changes and told me that I looked much better and rested. But we did not make any decision about tomorrow's agenda at that time. After eating the snacks I went back to my room to sleep.

At dinner time I was back in the dining room. There were other trekkers too. Most of them were exhausted and we started sharing our experiences of the trek and various other related things. Though we all came from various countries, background and age, we all felt like one family with a mission to reach the Everest Base Camp. As we were sharing our experiences, one of the younger trekkers said that he heard about a man who was about 60 years old, who had undergone quadruple cardiac bypass and was heading towards Base Camp. He wondered how crazy that man would be to undertake such a trek with his age and heart conditions. Hearing this, I smiled and responded that I know that crazy old guy and it was I. The young trekker could not believe it. He was surprised that I looked younger and also did not look like a person who had cardiac problems. As the young trekker was not convinced, I showed him my driver's License to prove my age and also had to zip down my shirt to show the surgical scar from the cardiac bypass. The others in the dining room were also curiously watching our exchange and some joined the conversation. Some of them wanted to take a picture with me! Inder and Pankaj were silently watching and enjoying the whole drama. Each and every one wholeheartedly wished me well and they wanted me to complete the remaining trek. After dinner I felt much better and normal. There were no signs of altitude sickness; I did not even have to hyper-ventilate. At this time I did not make a decision to continue the trek the next day to Gorak Shep — the last stop before the Base Camp.

I went to my room and started thinking over the past Two days experiences. My thoughts were loud and clear. I realized that I had a very close call with Death. In the event of anything happening to me, I would have put Inder and Pankaj in a quandary. I took my diary and wrote in bold letters:

My First Stupid Move---Will Not Repeat It Again

I also decided it is time for me to write a will and also to leave clear instructions in the event of my death. Lying on the bed, I decided on the details of the will, which I planned to draft immediately before proceeding with the trek further.

I summoned Inder and Pankaj to my room and informed that I had decided on drafting a will that should be followed by them in the event of my death. I put the wishes of mine in writing. I took my diary and wrote:

106

Living Will of This Trip
In The Event of My Death
Please Bury/Cremate/Anything Locals do
Do Not Send Body to USA or India
Just Send My Death certificate To My Wife in USA.
Written By Own Accord
Malur Vijay _____ Signed
Witness — Inder _____ Signed
Pankaj _____ Signed
Attn.: Kumar Basnet, Parikrama Trekking.

I made them sign the will as witnesses. After that, I told them in detail that these were my last wishes. After that I told them the details of the cash I was carrying with me: There were 500 US Dollars, Rs. 10000 Indian Rupees, and Rs. 20000 Nepali Rupees. They were free to use the money for necessary ceremonial rituals, including all their expenses. Any left over money, along with my death certificate, should be sent to my wife. Both of them were very silent and serious during the whole process.

An immense feeling of peace came over me. Every experience leaves a mark on us. Every mark is new and nothing is old. The past two days' experience caused all my old marks to vanish. The brain, the container of all experiences, was completely at bliss and peaceful with no thoughts but it was sensitive. I completely experienced the strong presence of "Now" the present by leaving the past and the future out of my memory. Sleep conquered me and I drowned into bliss and peace.

I wrote this on 14th May as I felt that I was nearing Death.

76

DAY SEVEN - TREK TO GORAK SHEP

In the morning of May 15, 23 after waking early before dawn, I could experience a great bliss and a strengthened body. It is very curious how mind and body coordinate with each other. The body was active. My heart rate and respiratory rate were almost normal. With the regained strength and energy I walked into the dining room to have breakfast and tea. Other trekkers too were gathered in the dining hall. Everyone was very happy to see me with the recovered energy. The last phase of the trek was treacherous terrain with lower atmospheric pressure, which attributes to lower oxygen availability. This phase of the trek is a challenge for a normal person. Considering my age and cardiac condition, everyone in the lodge was concerned that I should make it up to the Base Camp and back safe.

After the breakfast and tea I told Inder that I was ready to proceed with the trek. Both Inder and Pankaj agreed that I had regained my strength and we all packed. However, we all knew my body might not hold on for long. As we move higher the terrain was getting harder and hazardous. At 7 am we started our trek towards Gorak Shep.

The terrain was getting tougher. I was becoming exhausted and needed to make frequent and longer periods of stops. The vegetation and greenery were becoming less. There were no trees only bushes. Whenever I found some bushes; I used to go near them and breathe to get as much oxygen as possible. There were no paths; we had to climb over the boulders. I stopped for rest after climbing every boulder. The altitude of Gorak Shep was 17,088 ft. and Oxygen percentage was 52%. The low atmospheric pressure and lack of oxygen were making my breathing more difficult. I was exhausted and started to have the similar experience as on the 5th day of trekking. My heart rate was rapid and uncontrollable. I was hyper-ventilating and could not control it. My legs and arms were fatigued to the extent that I had to stop and rest after climbing every boulder. I sat on a boulder and started meditation. I went into a subconscious state within a few minutes, under normal circumstances I would have taken about 15 to 30 minutes. At this point I was having an Out-of-Body experience, once again had a close encounter with my old best friend 'DEATH'.

On seeing DEATH in front of me, I wanted him to relieve me of this body and take me away with Him. Death said that my time has not yet come and he cannot take me with him. Death was adamantly asking me to go back and end this trip if not to face the ultimate consequences. I was equally stubborn saying I would rather leave this physical body but would not go back. Finally Death said it is not my time yet to leave the physical body. Suddenly there was a lightning like feeling in my body. There was a strong silence everywhere, the body and the mind were motionless. This conversation with Death yielded purity and peace. I realized at this point that I would certainly make it up base camp with all my physical disabilities.

At that very minute I felt a sense of absolute nothingness. There was nothing that could make me afraid of anything. There was nothing that could disturb my heart and soul. There was nothing there that could take away my bliss and tranquility. Such was the absolute nothingness experience.

There was such a Bliss in that Nothingness. "I" did not exist.

There was no "I", There was no "My".

There was just **"Nothing"**, in that **Nothingness Everything existed**. Such was the purity of that **Nothingness**. "It Was Absolute Bliss"

I realized from that moment my life would be simple *"Absolute Living"*.

I felt that I am not just a physical body but also **ONE** with the **UNIVERSE**.

I could experience being **ONE** in the *"Universality of the Universe"*.

I came out of my meditation with a renewed vigor and energy. I do not know whether this experience was an illusion, hallucination or Out-of-Body experience. Inder and Pankaj were sitting on a boulder opposite me and were watching me intensely. Pankaj with a smile said I looked energized. Inder wanted us to move forward as we had almost 2 hours of trekking ahead of us.

We started to trek. From this point I was free from fears, hopes and despairs of past or future, contradictions of human beings and its own self-centered activities. As I was trekking I looked around the mountain and stood still with the intense beauty of the world. At that moment, the very majesty of the mountains made me forget myself 'I' did not exist, only grandeur existed.

As I was watching the snowcapped mountains, I imagined that Mother Nature was traveling in the sky with a basket lull of jasmine flowers. She took out a handful of flowers and sprinkled them around, every flower turned into a snowcapped mountain.

On our way we came across another group of trekkers. We stopped and looked at each other. There was nothing to say, no words to utter. The beauty of nature was so intense and mesmerizing that we just communicated in silence, engrossed in admiring the Mighty Mountains. The silence was broken by one of trekkers, who said, 'Is there any way this beauty can be explained to anyone except to experience it?' That was a true statement. I was moving along slowly getting exhausted.

I kept repeating to myself that tomorrow I would be at the Base Camp Mount Everest. The very thought of the Base Camp made me move ahead with determination combined with a calm and blissful spirit. We stopped more often to rest. I kept wondering whether my fatigue and exhaustion were due to my age and cardiac problems or do the younger trekkers too have to undergo the same amount of physical strain.

As we were walking, there was complete silence inwardly and outwardly, in this intense and peaceful state of mind. I felt that mountains were trying to convey to me the message that we human beings should destroy hatred, jealousy and vengeance. To destroy them we must first identify and dissociate ourselves from all those thoughts. If every individual changes, it would be a better world.

We kept on trekking. The last half hour of the trek was not as treacherous as before. We reached Gorak Shep at 4:30 p.m., our last destination before MEBC. We went straight into the lodge, had a hot cup of lemon tea which provided us with some energy. Before dinner met the other trekkers who were all tired and relaxing over tea and snacks.

Everyone's face reflected a feeling of satisfaction on reaching this point and surviving the ordeals of the trek.

During dinner Inder wanted to know whether I wanted to proceed towards Base Camp the next day, I informed him that I would decide tomorrow morning after resting. In the dining hall many trekkers who had heard about me, were kind enough to come to conversation on how I had been doing. There was a nurse and a medical student among the trekkers. I wanted them to take my pulse and compare it with others. When they did, it was a big surprise that my pulse rate was still lower than the other trekkers. I noticed that my heart rate and respiration were almost normal. But it would drastically become erratic once I did any kind of physical movement. After dinner I went to my room. I could not sleep that night even though I was exhausted physically. I was still hyper-ventilating and had other symptoms of Altitude Sickness.

Around midnight I felt the urge to watch the moon. Wearing my trekking boots, I walked into the courtyard.

The moon was up in the sky over the mountains, it was huge and bright. It was a soft, quiet and peaceful night. The whole yard seemed to be lighted from within; the light from the moon was soft with milky white light. I stood there bewitched in the moonlight. Time stopped and beauty took over with all love and bliss. A movement of a yak trying to get up brought me down to the physical world. I went to bed, sleep was nowhere in sight. I could not sleep that night even though I was exhausted physically. I was still hyper- ventilating and still had other symptoms of Altitude Sickness.

DAY EIGHT - REACHING FINAL DESTINATION

We left Gorak Shep at 6 am on May 16, 2003, along with another trekking party. As we continued on our trek I realized that I wasn't able to keep up with the other group. I bid adieu to them wishing them the best and promising to meet them at the base camp. Now our trekking party was all by itself. The altitude kept increasing and the air became thinner. I was finding it harder now to walk at a brisk pace. I had slowed down considerably though the heart was beating rapidly.

As I went on walking, my heart rate increased, and my breathing was shallow and rapid. My legs were tiring very easily. After an hour I reached a state of steady but slow walking. I tried to regulate my speed according to my heart rate, breathing and support. It was like driving a vehicle in the automatic cruise control. I felt more comfortable at the regulated pace.

Inder and Pankaj were having a close watch on me; they frequently kept inquiring whether I am doing all right. I assured them that I would inform them if I felt completely exhausted. As we progressed slowly and steadily, we had a surprise. Suddenly from nowhere winds started blowing. The wind was wicked. This wind brought the temperature steeply down in a matter of seconds. The cold became unbearable. At times due to windy gust we took refuge behind large boulders. Mother Nature was challenging me at every step, which made me realize more and more that human beings have a long way to go on learning to co-exist with Nature.

At this altitude of 17,800 feet there was hardly any greenery around, only a few bushes here and there. As we continued our trek the thought of me not preparing adequately gnawed my heart. I chided myself for not carrying oxygen cylinders given the cardiac condition. What was

I, a cardiac patient doing at 17800 feet with no oxygen cylinder? As a trained medical doctor I should have anticipated the need for oxygen at this altitude with my heart problems. It never occurred to me how scarce oxygen is at this altitude because of the lower atmospheric pressure; at this point I could appreciate how ignorance can turn into bliss.

Whenever I came across some green bushes or greenery, I rested near them as I could breathe better. I have no words to explain what a change that minimal amount of oxygen did to my body. I do not know whether the greenery provided any miniscule oxygen or it was just my hallucination. However the fact is that I felt better. I was very thankful for the small plants for providing me comfort during the trek whenever I needed it the most. This situation makes me realize that we the human beings take Mother Nature for granted. We race through life without taking time to notice what has been provided for us, until of course it is taken away or stripped from our consciousness.

Regulating my Heart Rate through Meditation on 16ᵗʰ May 2003.

As we were slowly walking, Inder pointed to a mountain opposite us. There was a landslide; I was dumb struck. Inder told me that it was a landslide of not more than a year old but it has not yet stopped. We could see the fresh white soil and granites everywhere around the mountain. This was the reminder of what some of surprises we can expect during a trek on the great Himalayan Mountain. The terrain was getting rockier, unpredictable and slippery. Even walking at slow pace was tiring and exhausting. It was worsened when I needed to climb a rock or boulder. As we progressed further my abdomen bloated with gas that made me feel uncomfortable. This condition is called High Explosive Flatulence (HEF). As I was consuming more water, I had to urinate often. The scenario around me was serene and beautiful but my eyes were set on Base camp and my priority was to stay alive.

After two hours we had covered one-half the distance to the base camp from Gorak Shep. Inder offered me a sandwich noticing that I was very tired and exhausted. Without any hesitation I grabbed it from Inder. The small sandwich gave me a lot of energy.

It reminded me of an article I had read on food wastage where it said "Up to one-fifth of America's food goes to waste each year, an estimated 130 pounds of food per person. The annual value of this lost food is estimated at around $31 billion. Roughly 49 million people could be fed by those lost resources, more than twice the number of people in the world who die of starvation each year." But so many people and especially small children die of starvation and under nourishment when food is being wasted by the privileged few. I wish one day as one community we eradicate the disease called starvation out of this world. If every individual can take care of a starving child as he takes care of his own child, this world would be a better place to live. If we all realize that every child is a child of God and it does not need to be our own biological child, we can make an impact on the future of this word and humanity.

We walked with no end in sight. I was exhausted and did not want to think about the Base Camp. All I wanted was to keep moving and avoid collapsing. The priority was to be alive and mobile. We were at the altitude of 18000 ft. With all the exhaustion I could not fail to notice the fact that we were walking above the clouds. I watched the clouds below me without a word or any thoughts. Seeing them without thoughts felt like a miracle where I could feel the creation.

After three hours I heard Inder asking me if I wanted to see Base Camp. The very fact that Base Camp was within our sight made the heart flutter. I was energized. I looked at the direction Inder pointed and found many tents, which appeared small and pitched. I estimated that it would take me an hour to get to the Base Camp. We were standing at an altitude of 18,440 feet. We had a descent of about 200 feet to reach the Base Camp at 18,278 feet. With the final destination so close I started walking with renewed vigor. After walking for almost an hour we crossed over a small bridge, and walked five minutes to reach the Base Camp hill. We were at the Mount Everest Base Camp at 10:30 am, May 16. 2003. As soon as we reached the Base Camp, I fell on my knees and thanked 'Sagara Matha' (Mount Everest) for bringing me to her safely. Then I hugged Inder and Pankaj. I expressed my gratitude to them for being there. I still didn't believe that I was there at the Base Camp alive and well.

Having reached the Base Camp I wanted to know whether there is a place to report and register. I walked into the very first tent I came across. There I met Ian, an American climber who was waiting for the weather to clear so that he could climb the peak of Mount Everest. Ian told me that there was no official register. Trekkers took pictures as evidence of their being there. He then went on to say that there was an Internet Cafe on Yak Shit Highway (note of humor) run by Mr. Tsering G. Sherpa and he kept track of everyone coming to the Base Camp. After taking many pictures at the Base Camp, we walked to the Internet cafe.

Internet Café at MEBC connected through Satellite.

84

Doctor on Call on May 16ᵗʰ 2003

I met Mr. Tsering G Sherpa at the Internet Café and stated the purpose of my visit to the cafe. Mr. Tsering G Sherpa stated that his record keeping had no official bearing. When I completed narrating my story, he was surprised that despite multiple cardiac bypass surgery I had survived and conquered the Base Camp. According to Mr. Tsering Sherpa this was the first time he had heard anyone with multiple cardiac bypass surgery-reaching base camp and it could also be a Guinness record. He then offered me some hot tea, which was a blessing. After tea he then went on to record all the details. I sent some emails to family and friends. Then I called my wife and father. Mr. Sherpa offered hot soup that I could not refuse. As I was leaving after thanking Mr. Sherpa for his hospitality, he said representatives from Guinness Book of World Records were to visit Base Camp the following day and that he would let them know about my feat.

Mr. Sherpa during our conversation referred me to Mount Everest Base Camp Hospital that was located 10 tents from his cafe. I decided to visit the hospital. In the hospital I met Dr. Linda who was from Boston, Massachusetts, where I had my sports medicine center. After talking to Dr. Linda, we met some trekkers who were ready to scale the peak of Mount Everest if and when the weather permitted. They had various questions on my health. What were all the difficulties faced during the trek etc. They wished the best and said may be I might scale the peak sometime in the future.

DESCEND

At 2 p.m. we decided to leave the Base Camp to return to Gorak Shep. Inder anticipated that it would take more than four hours to go back to Gorak Shep given my fatigue. Before leaving the base camp at 2:30 p.m., I wanted to pay my parting salutations and respect to Mount Everest. I knelt down, with both my hands picked up water from a stream flowing, thanked "Sagara Matha" for protecting me, sprinkled the water on my head as a token of blessings. I also prayed that she should protect us and guide us back home safe. We started to leave the Base Camp to trek towards Gorak Shep. I found it difficult to walk away from the Base Camp. It took us 7 days of hard trekking and many varied experiences to reach the Base Camp and it was time already to leave the Base Camp.

I left the Base Camp with a heavy heart. The trek towards Gorak Shep was becoming difficult. The heart rate was rapid and breathing shallow and in addition to it, High Explosive Flatulence (HEF) or High Altitude Flatulence (HAF) was making me uncomfortable. My legs were very tired and I had difficulty standing. I also feared that I might have damaged my heart further.

Though I had all these suffering at the physical level, the soul in me was very calm and peaceful. As I was feeling physically very exhausted I knew it was time for me to sit and meditate which would rejuvenate me.

With this thought in mind, I sat on a flat boulder and started to meditate. First thing was to control my heart rate that was high and to regulate my respiration to a deep, rhythmic and slow breathing. I could reach the subconscious level within no time.

As I was in my subconscious state, I had the following interesting conversation with Mighty Mountain. Mountains asked me if I was Alive

When I answered "Yes" it wanted to know whether I am still living in the past and believe in future.

I replied past is gone, the future is still not here. I just live in this moment, now and only 'NOW' exists. The Present is very living and eternal. Mountains wanted to know whether I am ready to die. I replied, I never die; death is for my physical body only, my soul never dies.

Mighty Mountains asked whether my soul is happy and wanted me to make one wish. I answered 'soul knows no happiness or sorrow'. My wish was to have a 'Still and Empty mind'. When the mind is still and empty it is free. This 'still and empty mind' does not mean it is static but it is always dynamic.

Only that mind can bring peace to the whole world. Bringing peace to the world in which we are all part is every individual's responsibility. With this response Mighty Mountains bid me farewell.

This experience provided me renewed energy with a great feeling of ecstasy and bliss. My heart rate and respiration were back to normal. After eating some snacks provided by Inder we departed the Base Camp.

As we were trekking I noticed a strange geological phenomenon, icicles coming up from underground and standing like tall, icy anthill, they were facing up again gravity. Seeing my astonishment, Inder explained that it was the underground water gushing out of a hole. When pressures increases it freezes in the shape of a fountain and that is the reason that it looks like a reverse icicle.

We began our trek; I had to climb about 200 ft. that we had descended while going to Base Camp. This part of the trek was making me tired. As we had made it about 100 ft., out from nowhere, a large boulder almost the size of a refrigerator landed 5 ft. away from where we were walking. All three of us were shocked and froze. Motionless we waited for more boulders to land near us or over us. But nothing happened for the next few minutes. Inder and Pankaj were shaken. This was the first time during the entire trek I could see panic in the eyes of both the young men.

Inder took control of the situation. He urged us to move faster and move out of that area at the earliest. As with the lone boulder flying like this we might have to anticipate a landslide sooner or later. For the next half hour we walked in silence. I started walking at a faster pace expending all my energy. No words were exchanged until were ached a 'safe zone'.

After reaching a safer area we stopped, we made certain that there were no signs of any landslide.

As we moved down, I came across many beautiful and astonishing scenes of mountains and valleys. I did not have any memory of seeing them on the way up, so I asked Inder whether we were coming back on the same route or a different one. He said we have only one path to MEBC. On the way up, my only goal was to reach the MEBC so I had missed many wonders of Mother Nature.

As I was trekking down, I got myself immersed in the beauty of mountains; with a slow and steady pace we reached Gorak Shep around 6:30 p.m. I was exhausted and very tired even after having my dinner at 7:30 p.m. I went to bed around 8:30 p.m. At that point, I was not certain whether I wanted to start down the next day. After a deep sleep I woke up at 3 am for no reason and walked out of my room into the yard.

It was a full moon night. The moon was up above the mountains. The horizon was filled with the milky white light of the moon. It was huge bathing the mountains with the clear milky white rays of light. Snow-capped peaks and the ground around me glowed in such brightness that one could not look around or at the moon with naked eyes. I had to wear my dark glasses to look at the moon. I thanked God for such a beautiful sight. There was peace beyond thoughts and feelings. It was just the moon, the earth, the mountains and I the observer. It was just silence. Everything around was completely still. It was this stillness that cannot be described: the bliss of the milky white light of the moon had permeated my being.

DAY NINE - DESCEND
TO PERICHE

Got up in the morning, May 17, 2003 with a peaceful bliss. After a good healthy breakfast, we decided to head down. My overall physical condition was almost normal though I still had certain symptoms of High Altitude Sickness. I felt I was strong enough physically for the downward trek and also I needed to get to lower altitudes. Moving to lower altitude would decrease the strain on my heart and possibly prevent further damage to my heart. We started to trek towards Lebuche at 8 am. The trek to Lebuche was uneventful, I was deeply immersed in the beauty of the mountains, and felt that the earth was heaven and heaven was Earth. We reached Lebuche at 10:30 am. After refreshments we decided to trek further down to Periche.

We reached Periche by 3 p.m. We rented a room in a lodge near the medical center. After refreshments I went to the medical center to attend a free advisory lecture for the inbound trekkers that I had missed on the way up. I was just curious to attend the lecture and also to meet Dr. Kristen. As I was walking towards the medical Center, I looked at the monument, smiled to myself with the thought that my name would not be etched on the cones. When I walked into the medical center, Dr. Kristen was relieved and happy to see me return. She could hardly believe that I did make it up to the Base Camp.

She was very much interested to hear my experiences — both physical and spiritual. After my brief narration she said I was one of the fortunate persons to make it up to base camp with the cardiac problems and with no oxygen cylinders. She invited me to join the advisory lecture; there were about ten trekkers for the lecture. Dr. Kristen wanted to share my experience with the trekkers. While addressing them, I told them the greatest lesson from this trek is to 'Respect the Altitude'. Advised them to drink plenty of fluids, eat well and above all listen to the body and intuition.

After the meeting Dr. Kristen performed a general examination on me. Everything was normal and she recorded the same in her file. Dr. Kristen took all information about me and said she would be passing the information on to the concerned authorities. We said good-bye and parted. After the visit to the medical center, we headed back to the lodge, had dinner and drifted into sleep as soon I went to my room. My physical condition had improved compared to the previous night.

DAY TEN - DESCEND TO NAMCHE BAZAAR

The following morning i.e. May 18, 2003, we left Periche for Tengbushe at 7.30 am, and reached the destination by noon. It was smooth trekking; I was feeling strong and robust. After lunch we decided to proceed to Namche Bazaar. We reached Namche Bazaar at 3.30 p.m. We checked into the same lodge where we had stayed end route; the lodge owners were happy and surprised that I could make it up to MEBC. After dinner I went to bed around 7 p.m. My overall physical condition was close to normal and greatly improved.

DAY ELEVEN - MOUNT EVEREST MARATHON CELEBRATIONS

On the morning of May 19, 2003 when I awoke, I felt good with normal heart rate and respiration. My overall physical conditions were back to normal. It was the day of Mount Everest Marathon Running Race celebration. It was a big festive event; the race would start at the Base Camp and end at Namche Bazaar The total distance of the Marathon was 24 miles. At 9:30 am, I walked to the town center, the finish line for the marathon along with Inder.

At the finish line there was a big gathering of many dignitaries, trekkers and school children. By this time by word of mouth, many people had heard about a man who was 60 years of age with cardiac problems reaching MEBC with no extra oxygen or medical help. As I was walking towards the finish line, I saw a group of people walking towards me. To my surprise they started to greet and congratulate me. It turned out that they were the Members of Himalayan Expedition Marathon Committee. During the trek I met a famous mountaineer of great repute. He being one of the members of the committee had told about meeting me and my experiences to Mr. Bikrum Pandey, The Vice President-Convener of the Chapter Extension and Coordination Committee of Nepal Mountaineering Association and also President of Himalayan Expedition Marathon Committee.

Mr. Pandey said he had never come across or heard of anybody else with problematic cardiac history having trekked to the Mount Everest Base Camp. "This could possibly qualify for an entry in the Guinness Book," he said. Mr. Pandey invited me to visit his office and home at Katmandu, which I accepted.

We all waited for the Marathon winner to arrive at the finish line. 60 runners from 6 countries had participated in the Marathon. The winner was Uttar Kumar Rai from Nepal who took four hours one minute and forty-four seconds. It was a great feat! The spirit of all the marathon runners stunned me. I congratulated Uttar Kumar Rai and took pictures with him. Bidding adieu to everyone, we left Namche Bazaar for Lukla at 2 p.m. We stopped at Jorsale for lunch and reached Lukla at 7 p.m. I was exhausted.

We checked in at a lodge. It was the time for celebrations as we had completed the trek back to Lukla. I invited Inder and Pankaj to join me in my room for a little celebration of our successful trek and safe return. All the three of us toasted with the Scotch Whiskey, which I had with me and thanked "Sagara Matha" for making the mission successful and safe. We recalled all the danger we faced, the excitements, surprises which we encountered during the trek. We could not help laughing loud when we all remembered the HEF (High Altitude Flatulence). After a couple of drinks we treated ourselves to a heavy dinner and hit the bed around 10:30 p.m.

Winner of Mt. Everest Marathon Race -2003.

FAREWELL TO HIMALAYAS – FLIGHT BACK TO KATMANDU

It was time to take the flight to Katmandu. After breakfast on May 20, 2003, we left the lodge and went to the airport. There I met Linda and Ian who were also flying to Katmandu on the same flight. It was time to bid adieu to Pankaj. We had developed an intimate bondage in these few days. Though he had started as my Sherpa for the trek, he became my adopted son by the time I had completed the trek. Pankaj too was sad to see me leave; he was with us at the airport till we boarded the plane. I gave him all the warm clothing that I had brought from the US. I parted from him with a heavy heart. The plane took off on time from the tiny runway with a downward inclination of almost 35 degrees. We reached Katmandu at 10:15 am. As I landed at the Katmandu airport I had an opportunity to meet Mr. Reinhold Messner. He was the first solo trekker to go to the Summit of Mt. Everest in 1980. After a brief introduction and exchange of pleasantries, I took some pictures with him.

Inder took care of my luggage and as we were exiting from the airport, Kumar and Raj greeted me with a warm and happy smile. I learned from Kumar that Inder had kept them posted all the time during the trek whenever he came across telecom facilities. Both Kumar and Raj were happy and excited that I had completed the trek successfully. Kumar accepted that they were never sure that I would successfully complete the trek with all my limitations. Kumar was very emotional when he made this statement. They were also happy that their trekking organization was part of this unprecedented mission.

We drove straight to the hotel and the first thing I did was shower, which I had not had for the past 8 days. I had told Kumar and Raj that I would like to rest the whole day after lunch and we could meet at 6 p.m. They had made special plans for dinner for me. Kumar invited me to his home for dinner. We drove to Kumar's house, where I met his wonderful family. His wife Raina was literally a 'Gem' as per the meaning of her name. Kumar had two children, a daughter, Sushma and a son, Sujan. I instantly struck a bond with those two. Raj was accompanied by his wife, Choden, a teacher in the local school. The dinner was a traditional Nepali dinner where food was served in copper utensils and dishes. We sat squatting on the floor and had our dinner according to Nepalese tradition. Prior to dinner we all joined hands, forming a circle and solemnly thanked God for having given this beautiful life and the food for the day. This is similar to the grace that is practiced in the Western world. Kumar said that forming of the circle and the prayer was a common Nepalese ritual.

MEETING THE PRIME
MINISTER OF NEPAL

Being a member of the YMCA international Cultural Committee, one of our activities at the YMCA was to bring children across the world together of cultural exchange programs. I had a great opportunity to carry the Peace Flag of YMCA to the places I travel. I had wanted to meet the Prime Minister of Nepal on behalf of YMCA International Cultural Committee, Richmond, VA and initiate a cultural exchange program between Nepal and YMCA International Cultural Committee, Richmond, Virginia, USA. After returning from the Base Camp, I was informed by the trekking agency, Parikrama Treks and Expedition, Katmandu, Nepal, that the meeting with the Prime Minister of Nepal had been confirmed.

On May 22, 2003, at 1 p.m., I was to meet the Prime Minister, Mr. Lokendra Bahadur Chand. I was excited, as this was the first time I was meeting a country's premier. Mr. Han Ghimare, Manager, Parikrama Trekking Company took me to the Prime Minister's office. After security checks we were directed to wait in the lounge. Exactly at 1 p.m., I was summoned into the meeting room adjoining the Prime Minister's office. After the preliminary greetings, we discussed cultural exchange programs between YMCA International Cultural Committee, Richmond, VA, US and the Nepal government and about my trekking experience. He congratulated me on accomplishing the trek to Base Camp after undergoing a quadruple Cardiac bypass surgery at the age of 60.

Our meeting came to an end after 30 minutes. He wished me all the best if I attempted to trek the Summit of Everest, and I departed after taking a few pictures with him.

The following day I visited Mr. Bikrum Pandey, the President of the Mt. Everest Marathon Committee at his office. We discussed various things. During our conversation he would be willing to collaborate with any trekkers with cardiac problems or any other limitations who would like to trek to Mount Everest. He also provided me with a letter of recommendation describing my adventure, stating that this may be eligible for an entry into the Guinness Book of World Records.

With all things coming to an end at Nepal, it was time to start back to Bangalore, India. I had wanted to travel by train that would provide me with an opportunity to see the countryside of Nepal and India. Unfortunately, I picked up 'Khumbu Valley Cough' that drained me, so I decided to fly back to Bangalore, India from Katmandu. On the hindsight, I felt fortunate that I did not pick up the Khumbu Valley Cough during the trek to MEBC.

The great journey to MEBC, which started as a pilgrimage, ended with many experiences and lessons. On reaching the destination, the Mount Everest Base Camp, I have started a new journey of my life.

Everest Marathon - 19 May 2003

Mount Everest Golden Jubilee Celebration

Ofc of the Chief Co-ordinator

To Whom It May Concern

This is to certify that I met Dr. Malur R. Vijay, M.D. from Richmond, Virginia, USA at Namche Bazar on May 19th 2003 on the occasion of Mount Everest Marathon which was organised to celebrate 50th Anniversary of ascent on Mt. Everest.

It was brought to our knowledge that Mr. Vijay has completed Mount Everest Base Camp trekking from Lukla to Basecamp in 7 days and 2½ hours.

Dr. Vijay further reported us that following further record was made by him at his age with such medical background:

1. Dr. Vijay is 58 yrs and 8 months DOB - 9-19-1944
2. He had cardiac bypass Surgery (CABG) of 4 blood vessels (Quadruple) in Dec 1998
3. He did the trekking solo and without any extra medical assistance or extra oxygen
4. He left Lukla on 9th May 2003 at 8 am and reached Mount Everest Basecamp on 16th May 2003 at 10.30 am

On the above information given by Dr. Vijay, we think that this may have been the First Record set by a person who have gone through cardiac bypass Surgery (CABG) of 4 blood vessels in the past which in our opinion may qualify him to be in the Guinness Book of World Records.

We wish good luck to Dr. Vijay.

Bikram Pandey
Chief Coordinator
at Namche Bazar in the Everest Valley

Date: May 19, 2003

'Nawakott Ghar' Sanepa Chowk, Lalitpur   GPO Box 105   Kathmandu / Nepal
Tel: 55 45 900 / 55 47 900   Fax: (977-1) 55 2 85 75
E-mail: marathon@MountEverest.com.np   Website: www.MtEverestGolden50.com

Letter from Mr. Pandey, Chief Coordinator, Mt. Everest Golden Jubilee Celebration.

PARIKRAMA
Treks & Expeditions (P.) Ltd.

G.P.O. Box. 7105, Thamel, Kathmandu, Nepal.
Tel. 977-1-410720, Tel/Fax: 977-1-418812
E-mail: parikrama@mos.com.np

Date: May 31, 2003'

TO WHOM IT MAY CONCERN.

This is to certify that Dr., Malur R. Vijay from Richmond, Virginia, USA undertook the trekking of Mount Everest Base Camp which started on 09th May 2003 from Lukla and ended on 22nd May 2003' in Lukla. It was an honour for us to organize the trek for him during the 50th Anniversary of ascent on Mt. Everest when all the Everest Summiteers had gathered in Nepal.

Through our guide and Dr. Vijay himself, we were bought to the knowledge that Mr. Vijay completed the Mount Everest Base Camp trek from Lukla to Base Camp in 7 days and 2 ½ hours.

Furthermore, such a record made by him at his age, was inspite of the following medical background:
  1) Dr. Vijay is 58 years and 8 months. His date of birth stands at 09-19-1944.
  2) He had Cardiac Bypass Surgery (CABG) of 4 blood vessels (Quadruple) in December 1998.
  3) He did the trekking solo, accompanied only by his guide and porter and without any extra medical assistance or extra oxygen.
  4) He left Lukla on 09th May 2003 at 8 a.m. and reached Mount Everest Base Camp on 16th May 2003 at 10:30 a.m.

On all the above informations given by Dr. Vijay, we think that this may have been the First record in itself set by a person who have undergone Cardiac Bypass Surgery (CABG) of 4 blood vessels in the past. This in our opinion and knowledge may qualify him to be in the Guinness Book of Records as the first ever person to do so.

Also did he travel around the country by road and visited places such as Pokhara, Lumbini, Royal Chitwan National Park, Janakpur and Daman enroute to Kathmandu.

We wish good luck and the very best to Dr. Vijay now and forever.

Bal Kumar Basnet
Managing Director
For: Parikrama Treks & Expeditions (P.) Ltd.

Director, Parikrama Trekking Agency, Katmandu, Nepal.

FEARLESS LIVING

Fear is the single most potent deterrent, which shackles human beings from realizing their true potential. We do not venture to try doing the things we hold dear to our heart due to fear. Loss of life, loss of loved ones, loss of money and material possessions, loss of social standing and reputation, fear of criticism and ridicule are the fears which hold us back, Fear scuttles our spirit thereby making us lead a life which is opposite to what we really want thereby making us frustrated and miserable. Fear only exists to be conquered. By conquering our fears we realize the untapped and vast resources within us which helps us to overcome the very fears, which at one time held us back. Once our fears are conquered the spirit in us is let loose from its cage.

I too had my own little share of fears: These fears existed when leading a successful life with all worldly possessions. Then one day everything turned Topsy- Turvy.

I was left with nothing. What happened to my fears? They compounded with the accident. Then I realized that these fears would stay with me as long as I was afraid of them.

Once I let go of these fears I felt as if a heavy burden was lifted off my shoulders.

I conquered most of the fears which hounded me by undertaking the trek to base camp. Now this doesn't mean everyone with fears should undertake an adventurous trip.

Everyone has immense strength and potential within themselves to overcome any fear. We have to tap this potential and strength.

The moment we realize that through life's lessons and experiences, would we learn that anything is achievable. This was a great experience of my life. It had made me a different person with a different perspective.

If MEBC can give this gift to me, I cannot imagine what wonderful experience I would have when I make an attempt to reach the Summit of Mount Everest.

Let's all...... "LIVE our life every day and die once".
Instead of ......"DYING our life every
day, and never living for a day."

Printed in the United States
By Bookmasters